THEY CHANGED THE GAME

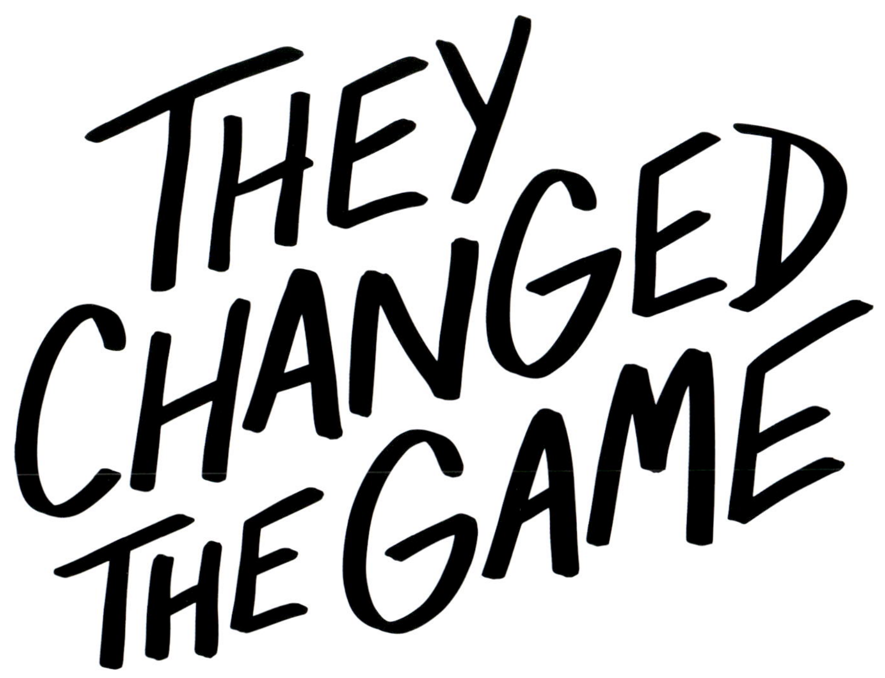

50 STORIES AND ILLUSTRATIONS
CELEBRATING CREATIVITY IN SPORTS

Matthew & Ariana Broerman

Library of Congress Cataloging-in-Publication Data available upon request.

This book is available in quantity at special discounts for your group or organization. For further information, contact:
Triumph Books LLC
814 North Franklin Street
Chicago, Illinois 60610
(312) 337-0747
www.triumphbooks.com

ISBN 978-1-63727-582-5

Editorial and Art Direction: Matthew and Ariana Broerman
Contributing Editors: Danny Cross, sports journalist; Paul King, sports journalist; John Moore, sports journalist
Cover art: Matthew Broerman
Book design: Ariana Broerman

Printed in China

To our families,
who may not have always understood what we were doing
but supported us anyway.

CONTENTS

9	INTRODUCTION	
10	ALICE COACHMAN	Track & Field
12	AXEL PAULSEN	Figure Skating
14	BABE RUTH	Baseball
16	BILL BOWERMAN	Track & Field
18	BILLIE JEAN KING	Tennis
20	BOB GIBSON	Baseball
22	CANDY CUMMINGS	Baseball
24	CASTER SEMENYA	Track & Field
26	CHUCK TAYLOR	Basketball
28	CURT FLOOD	Baseball
30	DAICHI SUZUKI & DAVID BERKOFF	Swimming
32	DARRYL DAWKINS	Basketball
34	DAVE VOLZ	Track & Field
36	DICK FOSBURY	Track & Field
38	DISGRACE OF GIJÓN	World Football
40	DOUG ALLISON	Baseball
42	ED WALSH	Baseball
44	FRAN TARKENTON	American Football
46	GEORGE MIKAN	Basketball
48	GREG PRUITT	American Football
50	HOMER JONES	American Football
52	JACKIE ROBINSON	Baseball
54	JOHANN OLAV KOSS	Speed Skating

56 **JOHN DEVITT & LANCE LARSON** Swimming
58 **JOHN MADDEN** American Football
60 **KAREEM ABDUL-JABBAR** Basketball
62 **KATHRINE SWITZER** Running
64 **KENNY SAILORS** Basketball
66 **KULSOOM ABDULLAH** Weightlifting
68 **LUDWIG GUTTMANN** Paralympics
70 **MAGIC JOHNSON** Basketball
72 **MARTIN BRODEUR** Hockey
74 **MICHAEL JORDAN** Basketball
76 **MIROSŁAW GRAF** Ski Jumping
78 **MUHAMMAD ALI** Boxing
80 **NUMBER 10** World Football
82 **PAUL BROWN** American Football
84 **R.C. OWENS & MORRIS STROUD** American Football
86 **RAY MANCINI** Boxing
88 **ROBERT WALTER JOHNSON** Tennis
90 **RODNEY MULLEN** Skateboarding
92 **SHAQUILLE O'NEAL** Basketball
94 **STAN MIKITA & BOBBY HULL** Hockey
96 **STEPHEN CURRY** Basketball
98 **TIGER WOODS** Golf
100 **TOM BLAKE** Surfing
102 **TOM DEMPSEY** American Football
104 **TOMMY JOHN** Baseball
106 **USAIN BOLT** Track & Field
108 **WILT CHAMBERLAIN** Basketball
111 **ILLUSTRATORS**

INTRODUCTION

BY MATTHEW BROERMAN

Like many ideas, it started with a sketch. Tiger Woods had just won the 2019 Masters, his first major in 11 years. To commemorate the occasion, I drew an illustration of Woods, red shirt, fist pump, with a Tiger roar. I asked Ariana for some impromptu feedback. We've been artists and designers for the past 20 years, and collaboration has always been part of our process. She pointed out a few things she thought I could improve, and the conversation naturally flowed from talking about the illustration, to talking about Woods, to talking about his influence on golf. Because of Tiger, courses changed their layouts, and competitors changed their training. Woods left a visible, measurable, and undeniable impact on the game. How many other sports were changed because of one player? The discussion left me questioning why the games I've watched my entire life are the way they are. How did we go from peach baskets to breakaway rims? From underhand lobs to 100-mph fastballs?

That night my mind kept me awake. The next day I posted the Tiger Woods illustration on social media, and Ariana and I picked up the conversation where we left off. I mentioned how cool it would be to combine the stories of game-changing athletes with awesome illustrations. This brought up the question: What makes a game-changer? Influence is hard to quantify—even in sports, where everything is measured. Our criteria: If you look at the game before and after an athlete played, is there a noticeable difference? Did the rules change? Did they pioneer a move or strategy? Would the world be different if they had never played? I checked back on social media. The Tiger Woods post had quickly become our most popular image and solidified that this was an idea worth pursuing.

We began our research. The internet abounds with rankings of the greatest players, but that wasn't what we were after. We were searching for game-changers, and more importantly, the stories behind the changes. What we found was innovation, creativity, and controversy. Players that pushed the boundaries of their sport, challenged long-held norms, and in rare cases, changed the game so drastically that you can't imagine it played any other way. We reached out to artists and writers from all over the world to help us bring these stories to life. We hope this book serves as an inspiration to fans everywhere and encourages them to be creative in whatever they do.

Alice Coachman

HISTORIC HIGH JUMP

Alice Coachman grew up poor in the segregated South of 1920s America. Like most kids, she loved to run and play games, racing barefoot down red dirt roads and setting up sticks and ropes to practice jumping. But her parents thought sports were unladylike, preferring Alice to stay home and do housework. They didn't think it was safe for a little Black girl to be running around backcountry Georgia. That didn't deter Alice. She would sneak off to the playground to challenge the neighborhood boys. "I was so tomboyish, I wanted competition," she said. If her parents caught her, "I got whippings, but I kept going." A neighbor once told her mother, "That gal's going to jump over the moon one of these days." Her mother replied, "Yeah, and she's gonna break her neck, too."

In 1939, Alice was given an opportunity to join the track team at Tuskegee Preparatory School in Alabama. She immediately began breaking records, winning 10 consecutive AAU outdoor high jump championships. World War II saw the 1940 and 1944 Olympics canceled, but in 1948 Alice finally got her chance at Olympic glory. As the London Games unfolded, Alice watched her teammates fall short of achieving gold. She realized it would be up to her. Coachman stood before 83,000 spectators in the high jump final and felt the weight of the moment. "I didn't want to let my country down, or my family and school." She rose to the occasion. On her first attempt, Alice soared 5′6⅛″, setting an Olympic record and becoming the first African American woman to win Olympic gold.

The King of England presented Coachman with the gold medal, and President Truman congratulated her at the White House. But back in her Southern hometown, racist views prevailed. At a ceremony celebrating her victory, the mayor refused to shake her hand, and Alice was forced to exit through the side door. "To come back home to your own country, your own state and your own city, and you can't get a handshake from the mayor?" She said it wasn't a good feeling. However, Coachman understood that her victory was part of a bigger battle. Through perseverance, she paved the way for future generations of African American women in sports. "If I had gone to the games and failed, there wouldn't be anyone to follow in my footsteps. It encouraged the rest of the women to work harder and fight harder."

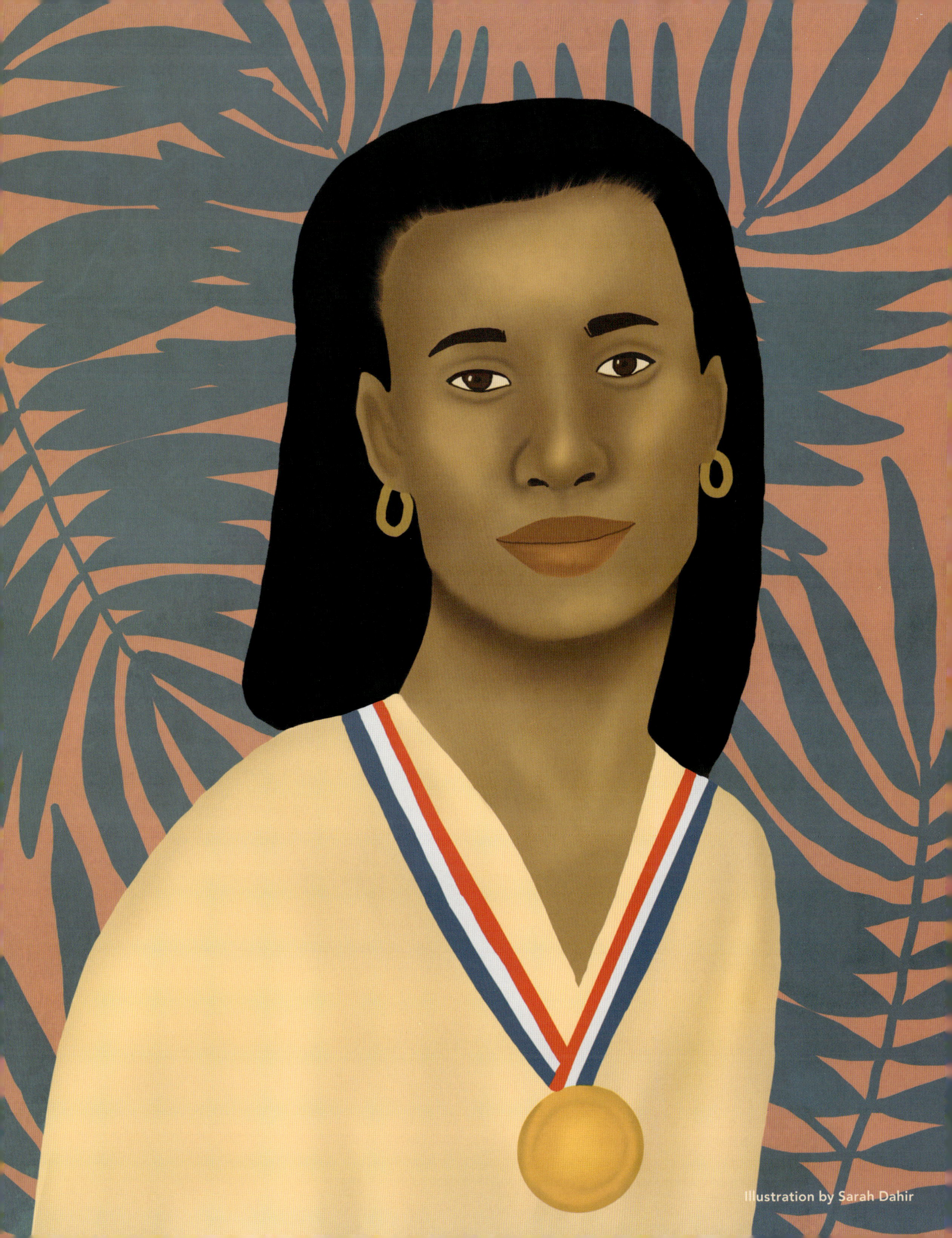

Illustration by Sarah Dahir

THE LEAP OF Axel Paulsen

Axel Paulsen was born in 1855 in the town of Aker, Norway. On weekends, his father Johan, a shop owner, took Axel and his siblings to the frozen Baltic Sea to practice ice skating. Johan was such a skating enthusiast that he had designed his own practice regimen, called "Paulsen's Catechism," which he required Axel and his siblings to complete when they went skating. Axel shared his father's love of the ice, and as he grew older, he journeyed on his own to the frozen sea to train each day before school.

In 1882, the first worldwide ice skating competition, the Grand International Skating Tournament, was held in Vienna. Many traveled to watch national skating champions compete against one another. Axel Paulsen had grown to be one of the best skaters in Norway, equally adept at figure and speed skating. At the tournament, Paulsen won the speed skating event, placed third in figure skating, and received a special prize from the judges for what they called "the leap of Axel Paulsen." Eventually, it would become simply known as the "axel." The new skill saw Paulsen leap from the ice and spin one-and-a-half times through the air before landing backwards on his skate blade. Axel's pioneering jump was made possible, in part, by a radical new skate design he had adapted from Jackson Haines, an American figure skater and ballet dancer. Instead of using straps to tie on the blade, the Haines design screwed the skate blade directly to the boot. The added stability played an important role in allowing Axel to land his aerial trick. After Vienna, Paulsen continued to compete in both speed and figure skating, showing off his new jump around the world. In 1883 he took first place in a race against 17 of the world's fastest skaters, and in 1885 he won both the speed skating and figure skating events in a competition in Hamburg.

Following in Paulsen's footsteps, pioneers Ulrich Salchow and Alois Lutz created their own eponymous jumps. For more than a century, these skills have formed the backbone of competitive figure skating. Modern athletes are pushing their jumps into rarified air, spinning three or four rotations before landing on their blades. It was Axel Paulsen who set off the jumping revolution, showing the world what was possible, and helping the sport of figure skating take a giant leap forward.

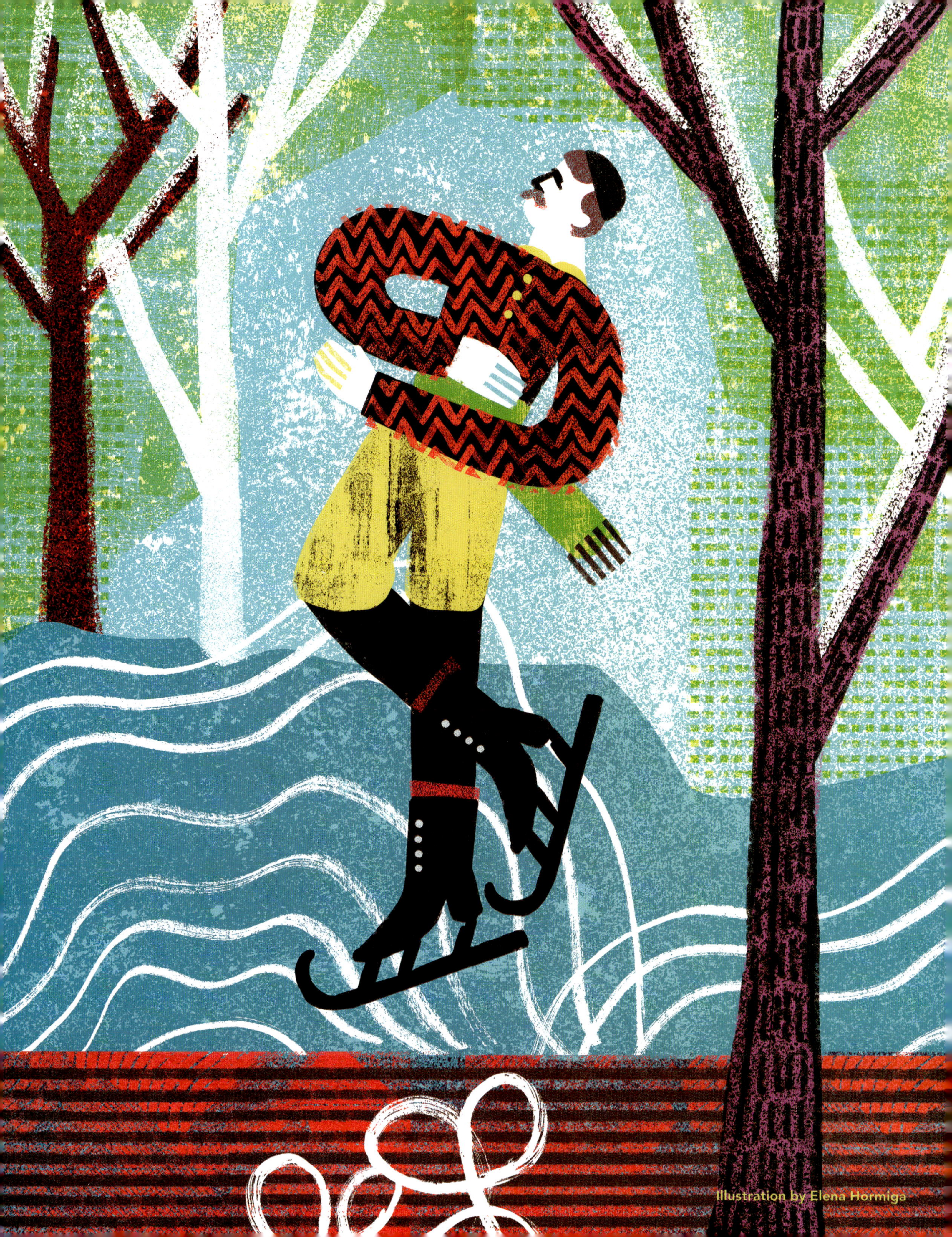
Illustration by Elena Hormiga

Babe Ruth

THE CELEBRITY ATHLETE

"It's difficult to convey to people today just how popular a sports figure Babe really was," said baseball historian Tom Stanton. "He's the most mythologized figure in American sports history." The myth of Babe Ruth rose out of America's roaring '20s. Coming off a victory in World War I, American pride was at an all-time high. Ruth embodied the American spirit, a boy who came from nothing to become baseball's biggest hero. He had a reputation as a stand-out pitcher who could hit the long ball. In 1918, he pitched 29 consecutive scoreless innings to help the Boston Red Sox win the World Series. In 1919, he slugged 29 home runs, breaking the MLB record and captivating fans along the way.

In 1920, the league took notice of Ruth's growing popularity and updated many of its "dead-ball" rules to benefit sluggers. That same year, Babe was traded to the New York Yankees for a record-breaking $100,000. Every paper in America published the story, and Ruth's celebrity hit a new level. Babe figured out early in his career that fame was a path to wealth. Sports historian David Voigt called Ruth "the most photographed of all Americans" during the 1920s. He endorsed numerous products, from candy to underwear. He starred in movies and vaudeville shows. He hired the first sports agent and became the first ballplayer to make as much money off the field as he did on it. All the while, he continued to slug home run after home run. In 1920, he broke his previous home run record with 54. The next year, he clobbered 59. Then he negotiated a record salary of $52,000 a year, more than double the previous record. He transformed the Yankees from a second-rate squad into a world-class franchise, leading them to seven American League pennants and four World Series titles.

For 15 seasons in New York, Babe Ruth basked in the limelight. He was the first athlete to effectively use the media to propel his myth. "Babe Ruth created the modern celebrity," said Ruth biographer Jane Leavy. From the rumor he ate 12 hotdogs between doubleheaders to his "called shot" in 1932, his stories are legendary and seem to get bigger with time. He was the Sultan of Swat, the Colossus of Clout, the Great Bambino. He was beloved by the media and the masses, and his influence on baseball and America was bigger than the man himself.

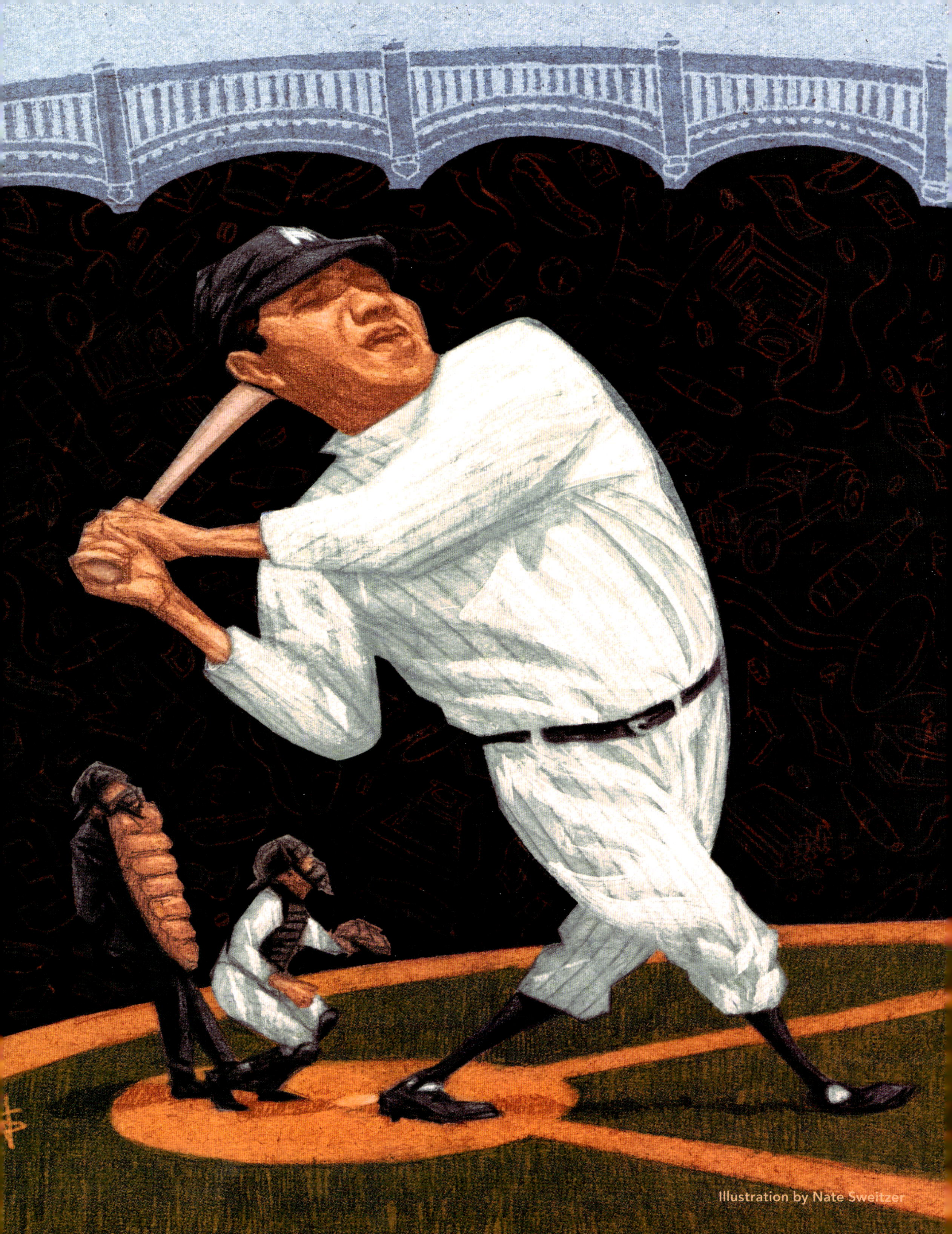

Illustration by Nate Sweitzer

Bill Bowerman

"A shoe must be three things," Bill Bowerman stated. "It must be light, comfortable and it's got to go the distance." Bill Bowerman knew a little something about shoes. In the 1950s and '60s, he was the head track coach at the University of Oregon, the place where track stars were made. He was constantly tinkering with ways to improve his runners' times, dissecting shoes and rebuilding them to be lighter and faster. He tried velvet, carp skin, rattlesnake skin, and kangaroo leather. In 1958 he made his first custom pair for one of his athletes, Phil Knight. Soon Bowerman was making shoes for more of his runners, cranking out new designs weekly and testing their performance. He sought partnerships with shoemakers, but none were interested. He wrote, "I now have the best shoe in the world—if I could just find some good American shoemaker to make it." That shoemaker was right under his nose. After graduating from Oregon, Phil Knight began working with shoe manufacturers and importing footwear from Japan. Knight approached Bowerman as a potential customer, but Bill suggested a partnership instead. With a handshake, the two friends started Blue Ribbon Sports, the precursor to Nike.

In 1971 Bowerman became obsessed with finding an alternative to metal spikes that would be lighter and provide traction on a variety of surfaces. One Sunday morning, his wife Barbara served him a waffle, and Bill thought, "What if you reversed the pattern and formed a material with raised waffle-grid nubs?" He raced to his workshop and returned with two chemicals to mix urethane. He poured the solution into the waffle iron, and his idea took form. Bowerman's kitchen experiment became the basis for Nike's Waffle Trainer, a shoe that revolutionized running and helped Nike grow into a footwear giant.

Bowerman's innovations went beyond footwear. Nike employee Jeff Johnson, who worked with Bowerman, remembered, "He challenged accepted notions of traction, cushioning, biomechanics and even of anatomy itself." He pioneered the hard/easy principle, the idea that an athlete needs time to recover between hard workouts. He invented the first artificial track, and his best-selling book, *Jogging*, inspired the running boom of the 1970s. Bowerman coached 31 Olympians, 24 NCAA champions, and 16 sub-four-minute milers. From the shoes to the training to the culture of running, Bill Bowerman pioneered it all. The wild ideas from "that crazy man," as Knight once called him, changed the course of track and field, shaped the biggest shoe company in the world, and inspired generations to go out and run.

"HE CHALLENGED ACCEPTED NOTIONS OF TRACTION, CUSHIONING, BIOMECHANICS AND EVEN OF ANATOMY ITSELF."

—JEFF JOHNSON, NIKE EMPLOYEE

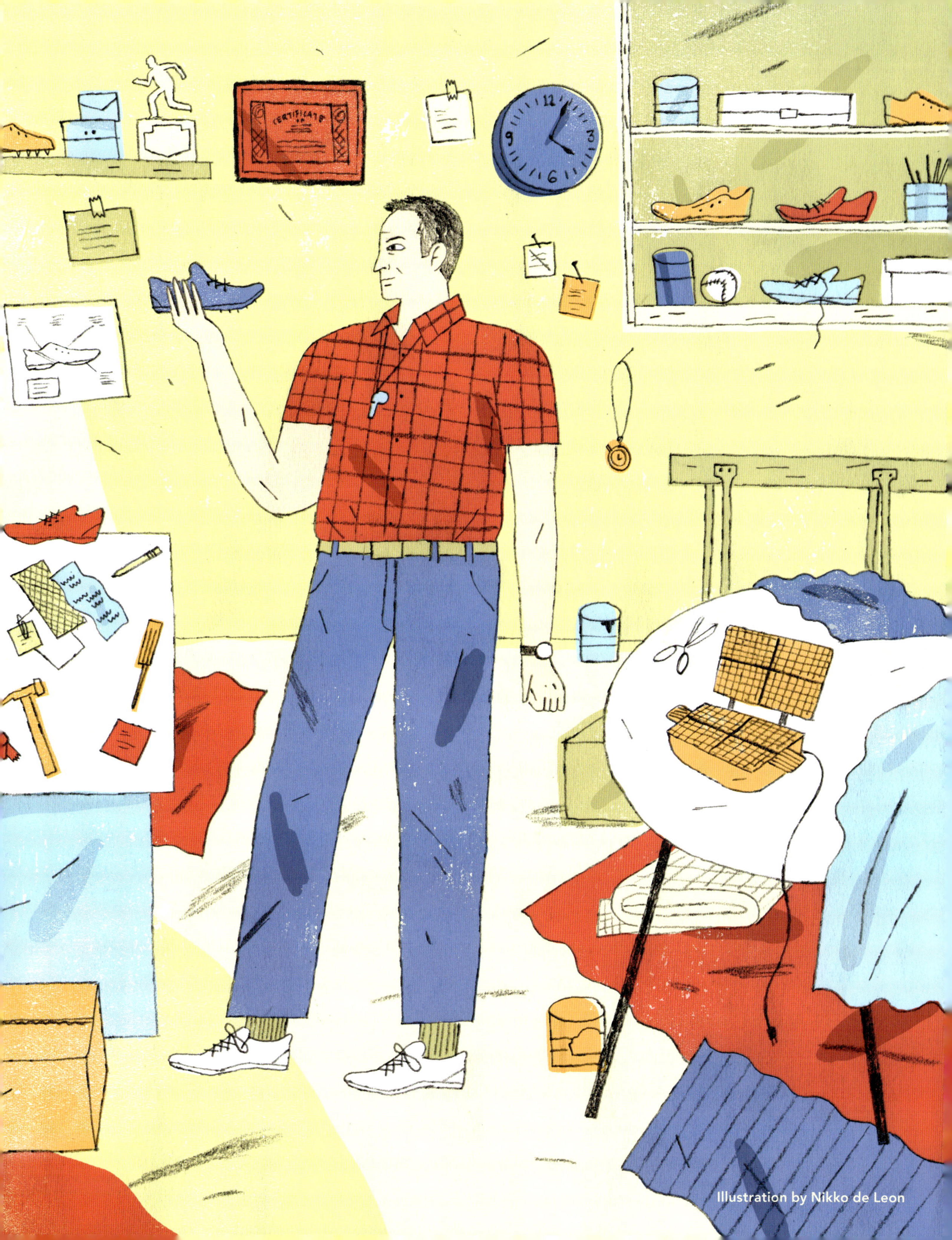

Illustration by Nikko de Leon

"I WANTED TO USE SPORTS FOR SOCIAL CHANGE."

—BILLIE JEAN KING

Billie Jean King

As a professional tennis player in the 1960s, Billie Jean King felt firsthand the inequality between men and women. In tournament after tournament, the men's prize was greater than the women's, and the unfairness disgusted Billie Jean. She made it her mission to right the wrong and knew that to be taken seriously, she would have to be the best. King said, "Unless I was number one, I wouldn't be listened to." After winning the 1972 US Open as the top-ranked women's player, she received less than half the prize money of the men's champion. Outraged, she decided to take a stand.

King threatened to boycott the tournament the following year unless the men's and women's prize money was the same. In 1973, the US Open met King's demands, becoming the first major tournament to award equal payouts to men and women. In September of the same year, King struck another blow for equality by defeating Bobby Riggs, a former number one men's player, in the "Battle of the Sexes." The match was televised globally and watched by more people than the Super Bowl. She understood the importance of her victory, saying, "I thought it would set us back 50 years if I didn't win that match."

For the next four decades, King continued to fight for equal pay and gender rights. She testified before the US Congress in support of Title IX, ensuring that anyone, regardless of gender, has equal access to federally funded educational programs, including sports. In 1973, she founded the Women's Tennis Association to provide equal opportunity and prize money for women in professional tennis. One year later, she founded the Women's Sports Foundation, an organization helping women reach their potential through sports, education, and advocacy. In 1990, *Life* magazine named her one of the "100 Most Important Americans of the 20th Century." She was the only female athlete on the list.

King's tireless efforts have resulted in greater equality and opportunity for women everywhere. It took 34 years, but in 2007, Wimbledon became the last major tennis tournament to award equal prize money to men and women. Billie Jean King's impact on the world is far greater than her record-breaking tennis victories. She said, "Everyone thinks women should be thrilled when we get crumbs, and I want women to have the cake, the icing and the cherry on top, too."

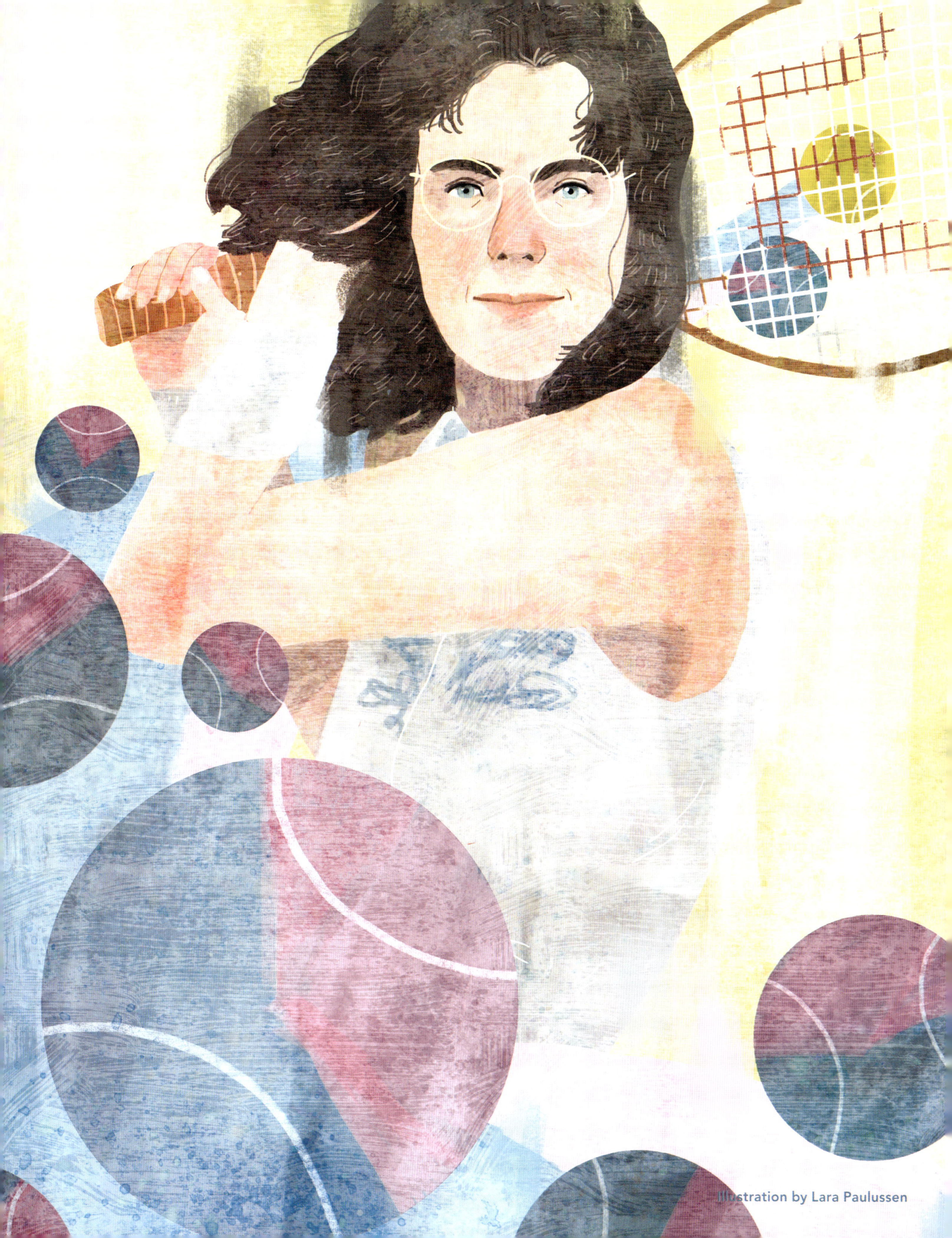

Illustration by Lara Paulussen

Bob Gibson

In Game 1 of the 1968 World Series, Bob Gibson stood high on the mound, teeth clenched, hat pulled low over his furrowed brow. Gibson looked angry. He pitched better when he was angry. That day he fanned six of the first seven batters, on his way to a World Series–record 17 strikeouts.

1968 was baseball's "Year of the Pitcher," and the best pitcher that year was Bob Gibson. He won 22 games, threw 13 shutouts, and led the league in strikeouts. Gibson was a fierce competitor—his best pitch, intimidation. He said, "The best feeling out of the whole thing is they didn't want to face me. No one wanted to face me." Opposing hitters feared Gibson, who wasn't afraid to hurl his 95-mph fastball high and tight. He'd follow the fastball with a slider that started at their heads and curved across the plate, leaving batters shaking. Hall of Famer Hank Aaron told Dusty Baker, "Don't dig in against Bob Gibson; he'll knock you down. He'd knock down his own grandmother if she dared to challenge him. Don't stare at him, don't smile at him, don't talk to him. He doesn't like it. If you happen to hit a home run, don't run too slow, don't run too fast.... And if he hits you, don't charge the mound, because he's a Gold Glove boxer." That year, Gibson recorded a 1.12 ERA, a mark that's never been matched in the "live-ball" era.

Major League Baseball thought pitchers like Gibson had gotten too good. Team owners worried that low-scoring games would turn off fans. In 1968, the league batting average was the lowest ever, with only six players averaging over .300. Right fielder Ken Harrelson said, "I remember 1968, it felt like every pitcher was right on top of you that year." For the '69 season, MLB decided to take a little oomph away from hurlers. The mound was lowered from 15 to 10 inches, reducing a pitcher's leverage, and the top of the strike zone dropped from the players' shoulders down to their armpits. The changes worked. In 1969, almost every major hitting category saw an increase. Even with the changes, Gibson continued to dominate. He won 20 games in 1969 and 23 in 1970, along with his second Cy Young Award. It turned out his pitching style wasn't dependent on mound height or strike zone size, but something else. He said, "The part of pitching that separates the stars from everyone else is about 90 percent mental. That's why I considered it so important to mess with a batter's head without letting him inside mine."

"DON'T DIG IN AGAINST BOB GIBSON; HE'LL KNOCK YOU DOWN. HE'D KNOCK DOWN HIS OWN GRANDMOTHER IF SHE DARED TO CHALLENGE HIM."

—HANK AARON, HALL OF FAME OUTFIELDER

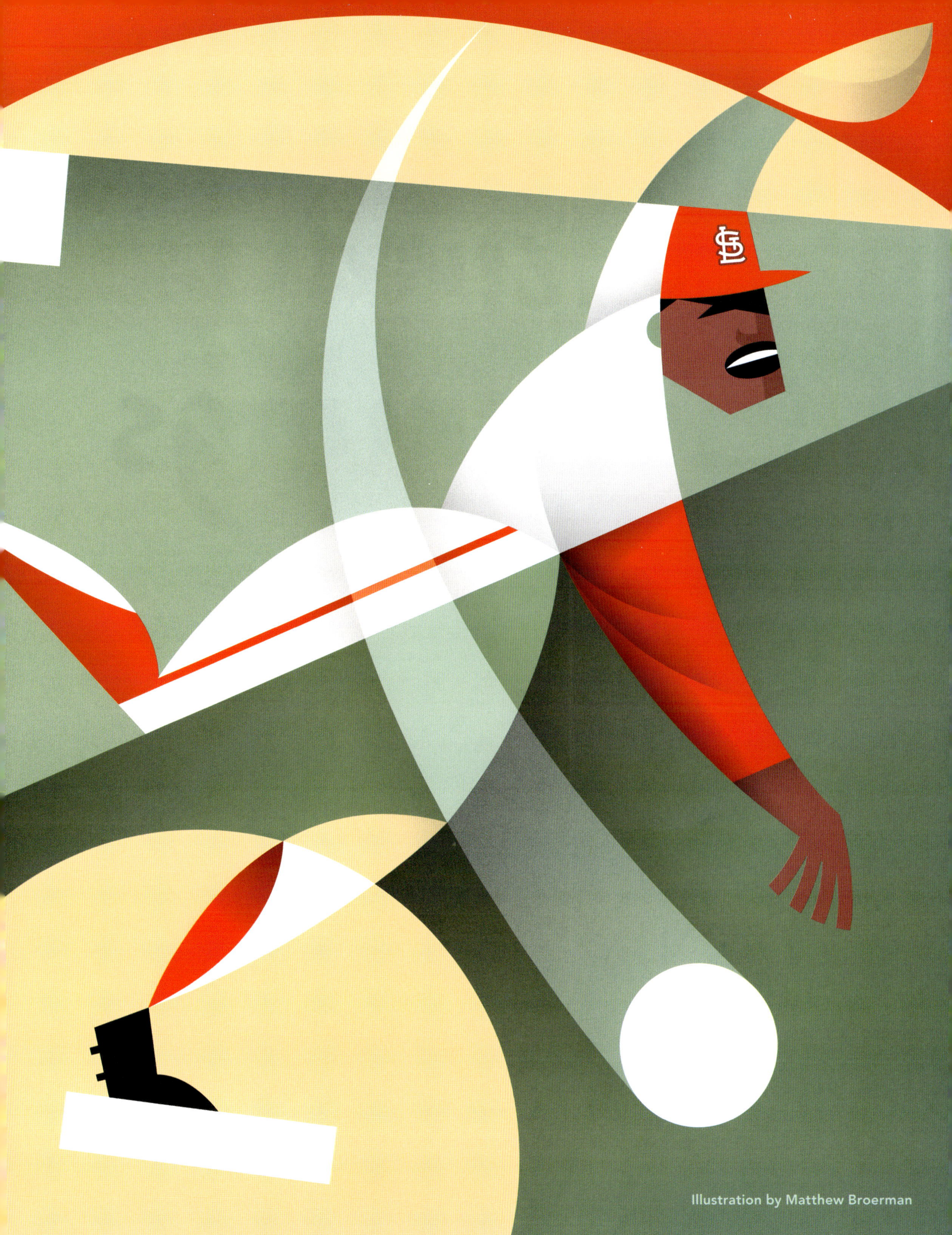

Illustration by Matthew Broerman

Candy Cummings

THE CURVEBALL

In the summer of 1863, 14-year-old William Arthur Cummings was playing with his friends at a Brooklyn beach. The boys were throwing clamshells, and they noticed how the shells curved in the air before landing in the water. Cummings was a promising young pitcher and thought to himself, "It would be a good joke on the boys if I could make a baseball curve the same way."

Cummings began experimenting with ways to make the ball curve, using different grips and arm motions. But he never felt confident enough to use the pitch in a game. Even without the curve, he proved to be a premier pitcher. In 1865, he joined the Star Junior amateur team of Brooklyn, posting a 37-2 record. Later that year, he was invited to play for the Brooklyn Excelsior Club, one of the best teams in New York. He quickly became their leading pitcher, earning the nickname "Candy," a term meaning the best.

Finally, after years of secret training, Candy decided to unveil his curveball. On October 7, 1867, in a game against Harvard College, Cummings hurled the ball with a quick snap of his wrist and a flick of his finger. "I began to watch the flight of the ball through the air and distinctly saw it curve.... A surge of joy flooded over me that I shall never forget," he wrote. "I tried again with the same result, and then I realized that I had succeeded at last." Since no other pitchers could throw a curveball, hitters couldn't practice against it. Baseball historian David Fleitz wrote, "Batters flailed helplessly at the new pitch." Candy was in the top 10 in strikeouts every year of his professional career, leading the league in 1875. That same year, he threw seven shutout games. Fleitz called him "the most dominant pitcher in the country."

Cummings transformed the role of a pitcher from someone who merely delivered the ball into a strategic player who could limit a batter's hitting. In the decades that followed, pitchers became more creative, adding the spitball, slider, knuckleball, screwball, and changeup. In his later years, he said, "I get a great deal of pleasure now in my old age out of going to games and watching the curves, thinking that it was through my blind efforts that all this was made possible." Candy's invention of the curveball earned him a place in the Baseball Hall of Fame.

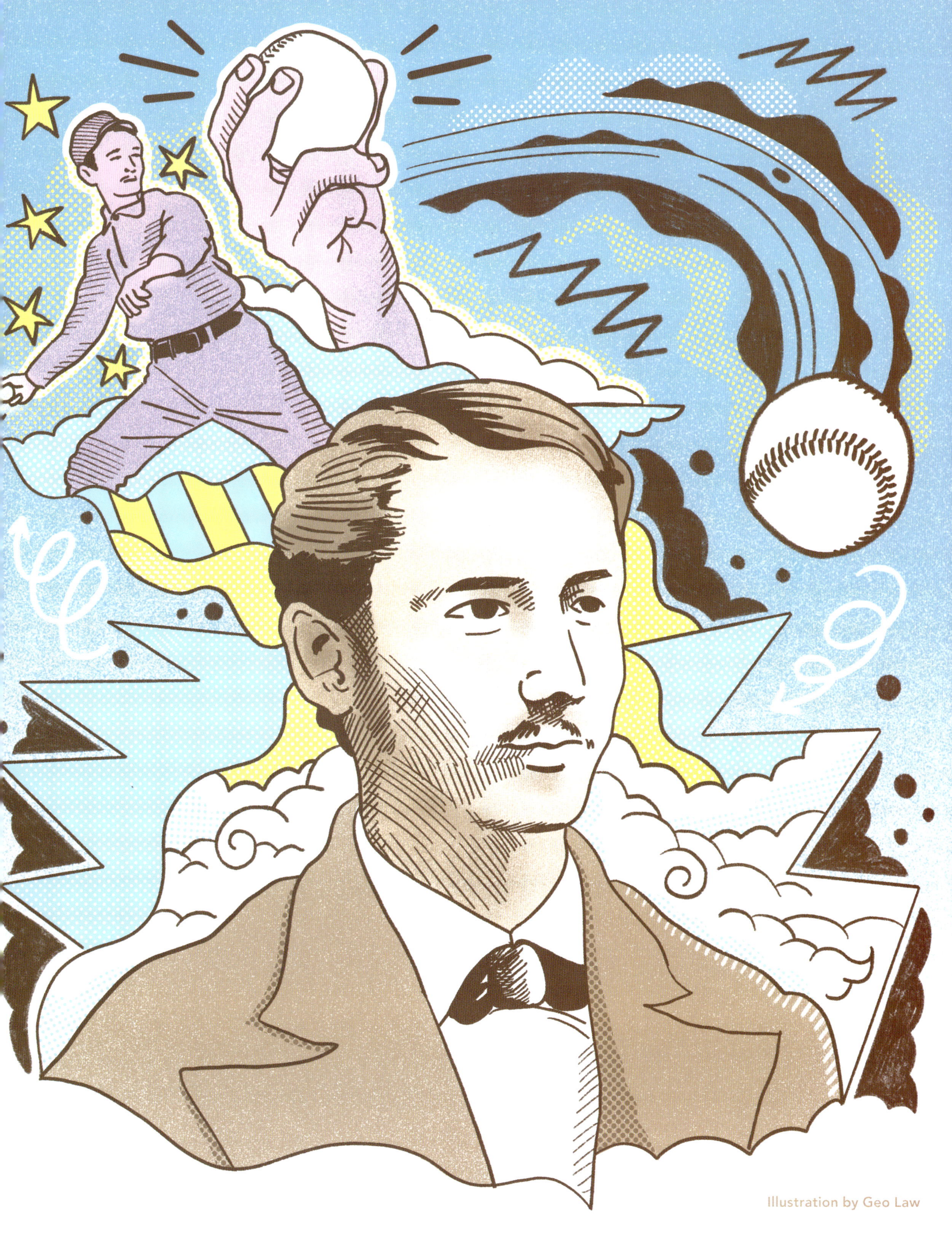

Illustration by Geo Law

"GOD MADE ME THE WAY I AM, AND I ACCEPT MYSELF."

—CASTER SEMENYA

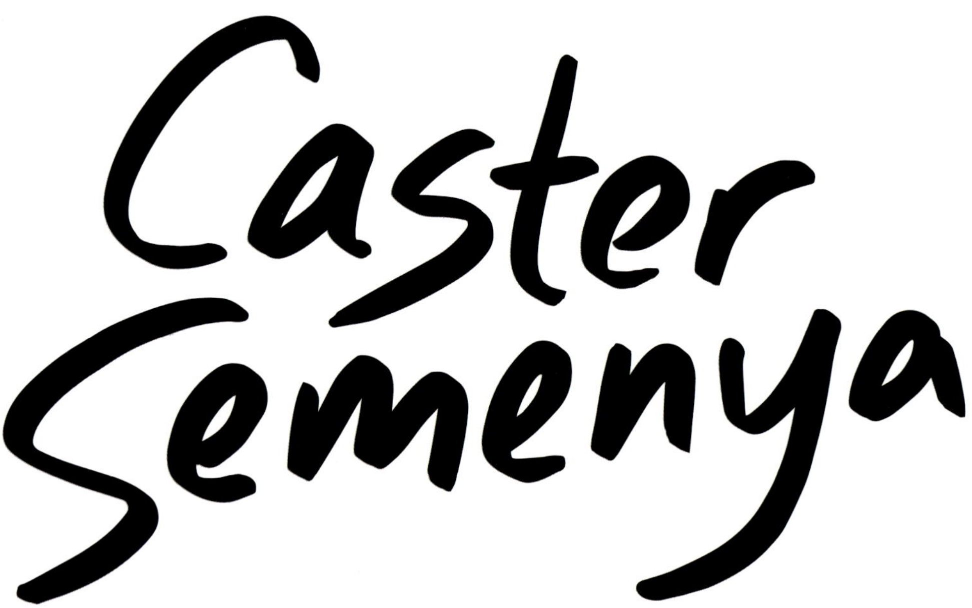

At the 2009 African Junior Championships, 18-year-old sprinter Caster Semenya dominated the women's 800-meters, clocking the fastest time of the year and beating her nearest competitor by more than four seconds. Her victory aroused suspicion, and the International Amateur Athletic Federation asked Semenya to submit to what she was told was a doping test. The test was actually for gender verification. The results revealed that although Caster was a woman on the outside, she had both male and female characteristics internally, including high levels of testosterone. Semenya was banned from certain events and forced into a decade-long battle about what defines a woman.

Gender testing in sports has a long history of targeting women who appeared too "manly." At the 1936 Berlin Olympics, muscular female sprinter Helen Stephens was subjected to a gender examination by German officials before she won gold in the 100-meters. For decades, visual inspections and physical exams were the primary methods of verification until chromosome and hormone tests were developed. Female athletes were forced into humiliating "nude parades" in front of doctors and officials who would then issue "certificates of femininity." The tests were demeaning, and the results often led to public ridicule. Semenya's results sparked a firestorm of controversy. Fellow sprinter Elisa Cusma said, "These kind of people should not run with us. For me, she is not a woman. She is a man." Pierre Weiss of the IAAF said, "She is a woman, but maybe not 100 percent."

In 2010, the IAAF cleared Semenya to compete. She won gold at the 2012 and 2016 Olympics, but her success continued to cause controversy. Polish sprinter Joanna Jóźwik raced against Semenya in the 2016 Rio Games. "These colleagues have a very high testosterone level, similar to a male's, which is why they look how they look and run like they run," Jóźwik said. "I must admit that for me it is a little strange that the authorities do nothing about this." Shortly after Rio, the IAAF announced new rules regarding high-testosterone females. To be allowed to compete, Semenya, and others like her, would be forced to reduce their testosterone levels by either taking drugs or undergoing surgery. Caster refused, appealing the new rules, saying, "God made me the way I am, and I accept myself." Her fight is one of many in the ongoing struggle to define gender. "I am very disappointed to be kept from defending my hard-earned title," she said of the changes. "But this will not deter me from continuing my fight for the human rights of all of the female athletes concerned."

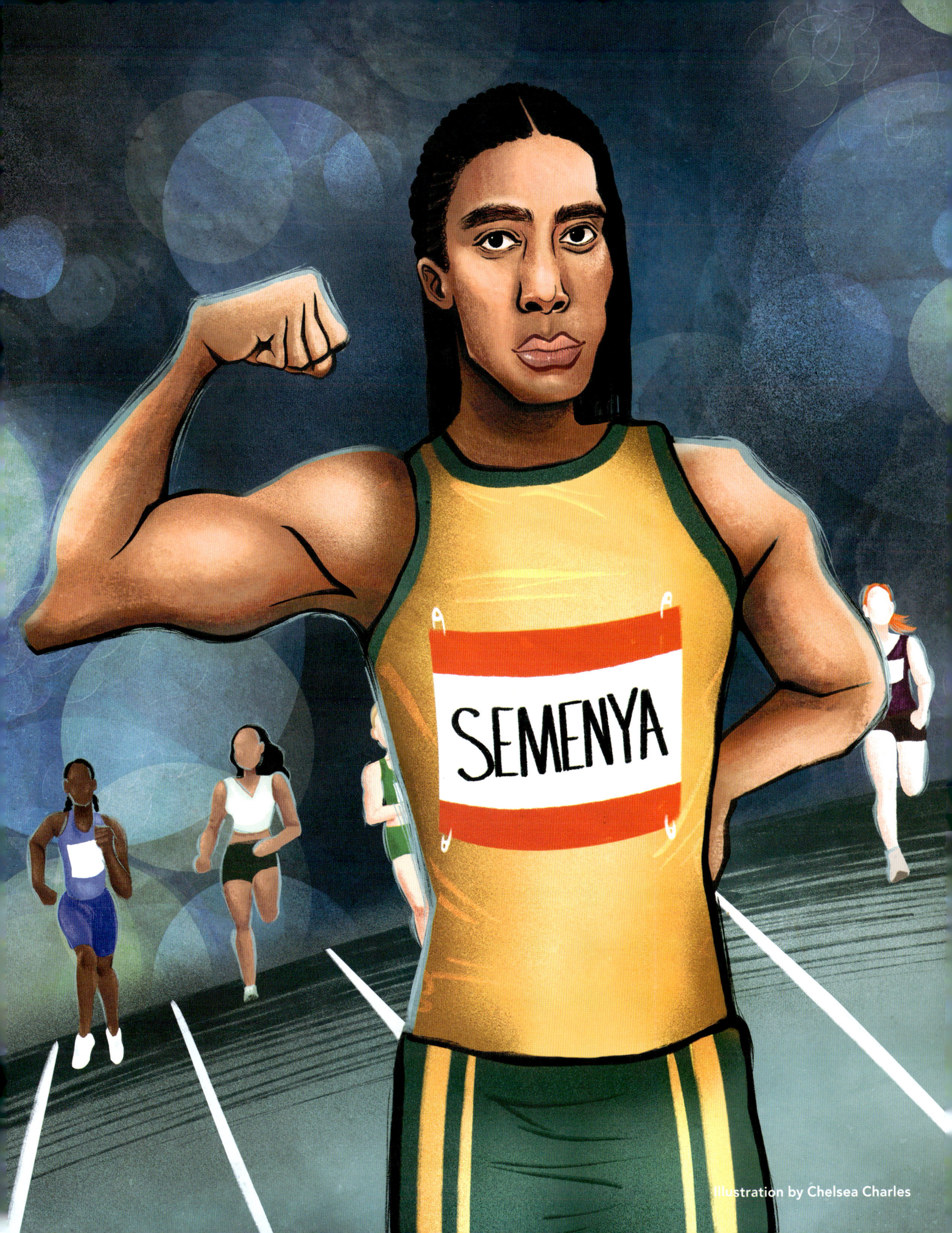

Illustration by Chelsea Charles

Chuck Taylor

THE SIGNATURE BASKETBALL SHOE

Fourteen years before the NBA was founded and fifty-two years before the Air Jordans, Chuck Taylor was the first player to put his name on a basketball shoe. The Converse Rubber Shoe Company began producing its "All Star" shoes in 1917, trying to capitalize on the rising popularity of a new game called basketball. But sales were slow. In 1921, they hired semi-pro basketball player Chuck Taylor as a salesman to try and grow the basketball business. Taylor traveled the country, putting on clinics and exhibitions. "He loved the game. He loved being a part of it," said Joe Dean, former Converse vice president. "He was a loveable guy and fun to be around and a nice guy, and he, at one point, knew every college basketball coach in the country." Thanks to Chuck, sales of Converse All Stars exploded. Customers kept asking for "Chuck's shoe" or "Chuck Taylor's shoe." In 1932, Converse made it official, adding Chuck's name to the All Star's ankle patch.

Converse's popularity continued to grow, becoming the official shoe of the Olympics and the United States Armed Forces. At its peak in the 1960s, the company had 80% of the total US sneaker market, and 90% of professional basketball players wore Converse. Taylor never asked for a royalty. Converse gave him an expense account and paid him by commission. He was on the road 365 days a year, living out of hotels. In 1968, Taylor retired from Converse after more than 40 years of selling shoes. He died one year later, and Converse began a financial skid. Increased competition from Nike, Adidas, and Puma, along with a series of poor business decisions, cost Converse most of its sports market share by the 1980s. But the company found unlikely success in a new market, becoming the shoe of counterculture artists and musicians. The shoes were simple, came in many colors, and were cheap. When asked about Chuck Taylor, Tommy Ramone, drummer for The Ramones, said, "He was maybe a basketball coach or something. I don't know. He made cheap shoes."

The Converse All Stars are the best-selling sneakers of all time. Worn by athletes, artists, authors, and musicians. Elvis Presley, James Dean, Dr. J, and Kurt Cobain all walked around with the name Chuck Taylor on their shoes. In 1969, shortly before his death, Chuck Taylor was inducted into the Basketball Hall of Fame, honored for his contributions to the game.

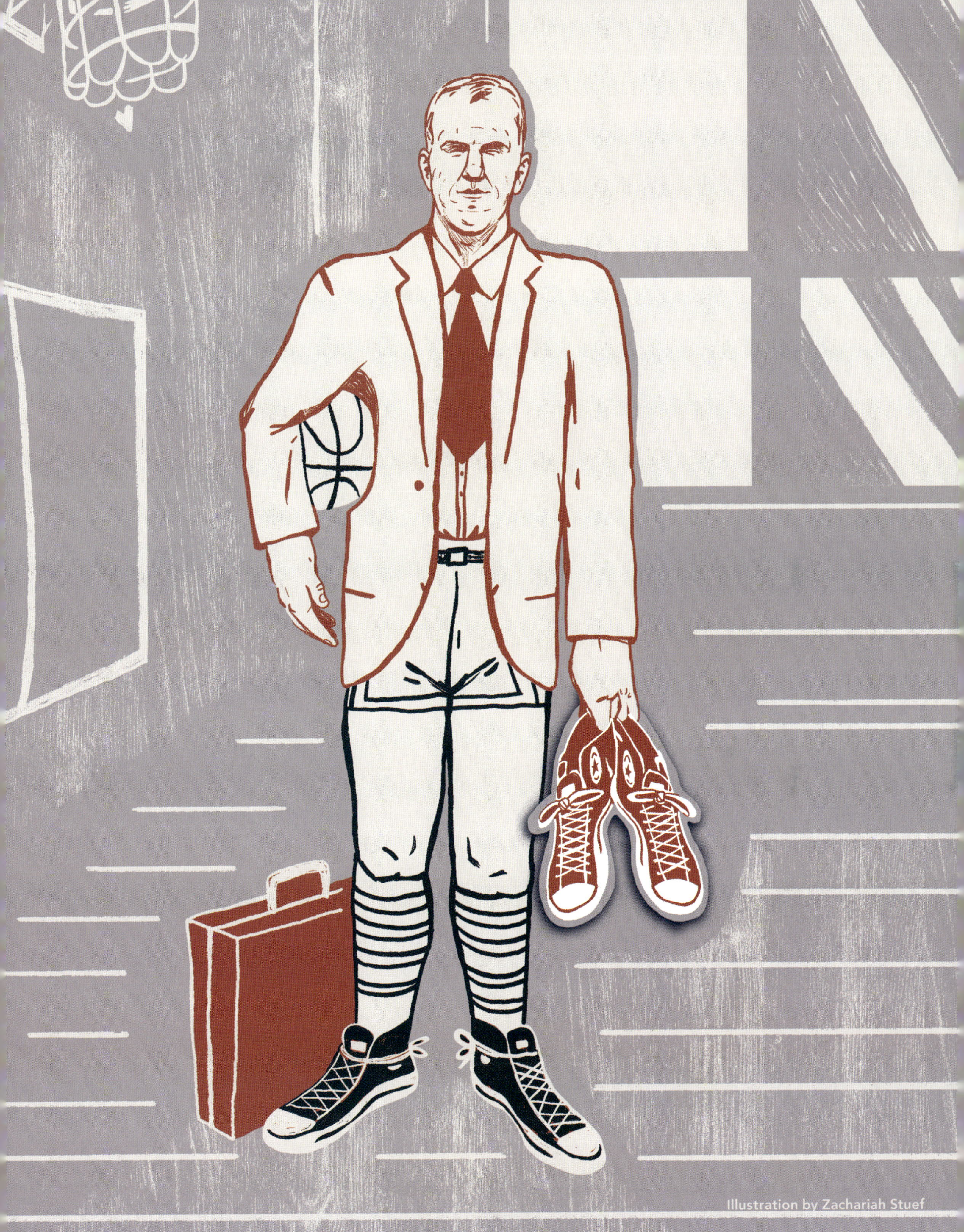

Illustration by Zachariah Stuef

"I DO NOT FEEL THAT I AM A PIECE OF PROPERTY TO BE BOUGHT AND SOLD IRRESPECTIVE OF MY WISHES."

—CURT FLOOD

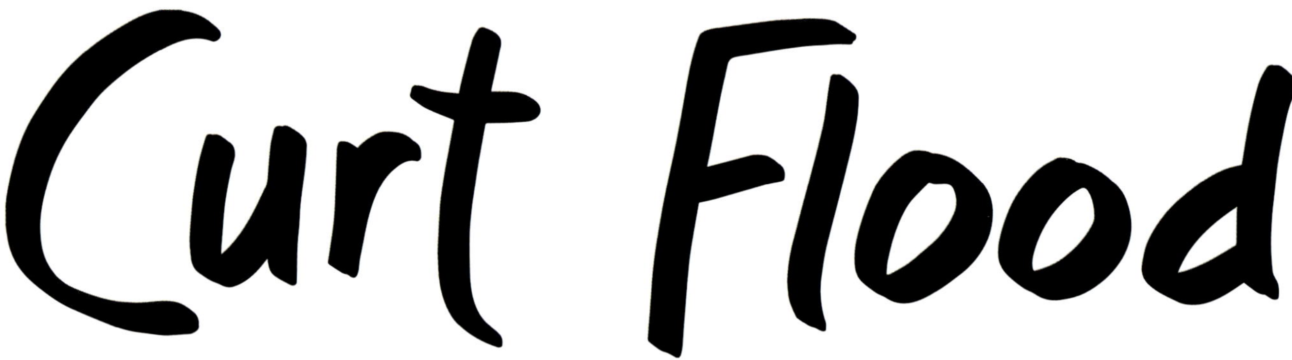

On October 8, 1969, after 12 seasons with the St. Louis Cardinals, baseball player Curt Flood was surprised to learn that he had been traded to the Philadelphia Phillies. Flood was a seven-time Gold Glove winner, three-time All-Star, and helped the Cardinals win two World Series. After everything he had done for the team, he told his wife it felt like "someone putting a knife in his stomach, or your mom throwing you away." Nobody asked if Curt wanted to be traded, or where he wanted to play. Flood wrote a letter to baseball commissioner Bowie Kuhn, stating, "I do not feel that I am a piece of property to be bought and sold irrespective of my wishes." Kuhn responded that he "simply did not see how that applied to Major League Baseball."

Because of the "reserve clause" in major league contracts, players were team property. Owners controlled all trades, sales, and negotiations. Players were bought and sold like livestock. Flood was active in the civil rights movement and believed the reserve system echoed slavery. Owners argued that if players could move freely from team to team, they would go to the highest bidder, and baseball would be financially ruined. Flood responded, "Unless I have misread history, we have passed the stage where indentured servitude was justifiable on the grounds that the employer could not afford the cost of normal labor." With the help of Marvin Miller, leader of the players' union, Curt Flood sued Major League Baseball. The case of Flood vs. Kuhn reached the Supreme Court on March 20, 1972. Flood ultimately lost in a 5-3 decision, but the high profile case and subsequent player strike sent Major League Baseball back to the negotiating table with the union. Miller and the owners reached new terms where private arbitration—not courtroom battles—would be used for contract grievances. Miller used arbitration to chip away at the reserve system. He encouraged pitchers Andy Messersmith and Dave McNally to play the 1975 season without contracts. At the end of the season, an arbitrator ruled that with no contract, there was no reserve clause, making Messersmith and McNally "free agents." The ruling undid 80 years of the reserve system and finally gave ballplayers the same freedom as other Americans.

Curt Flood never benefited from the movement he started, but all players since owe their liberty to him. Civil rights leader Jesse Jackson said, "Baseball didn't change Curt Flood. Curt Flood changed baseball. He fought the good fight."

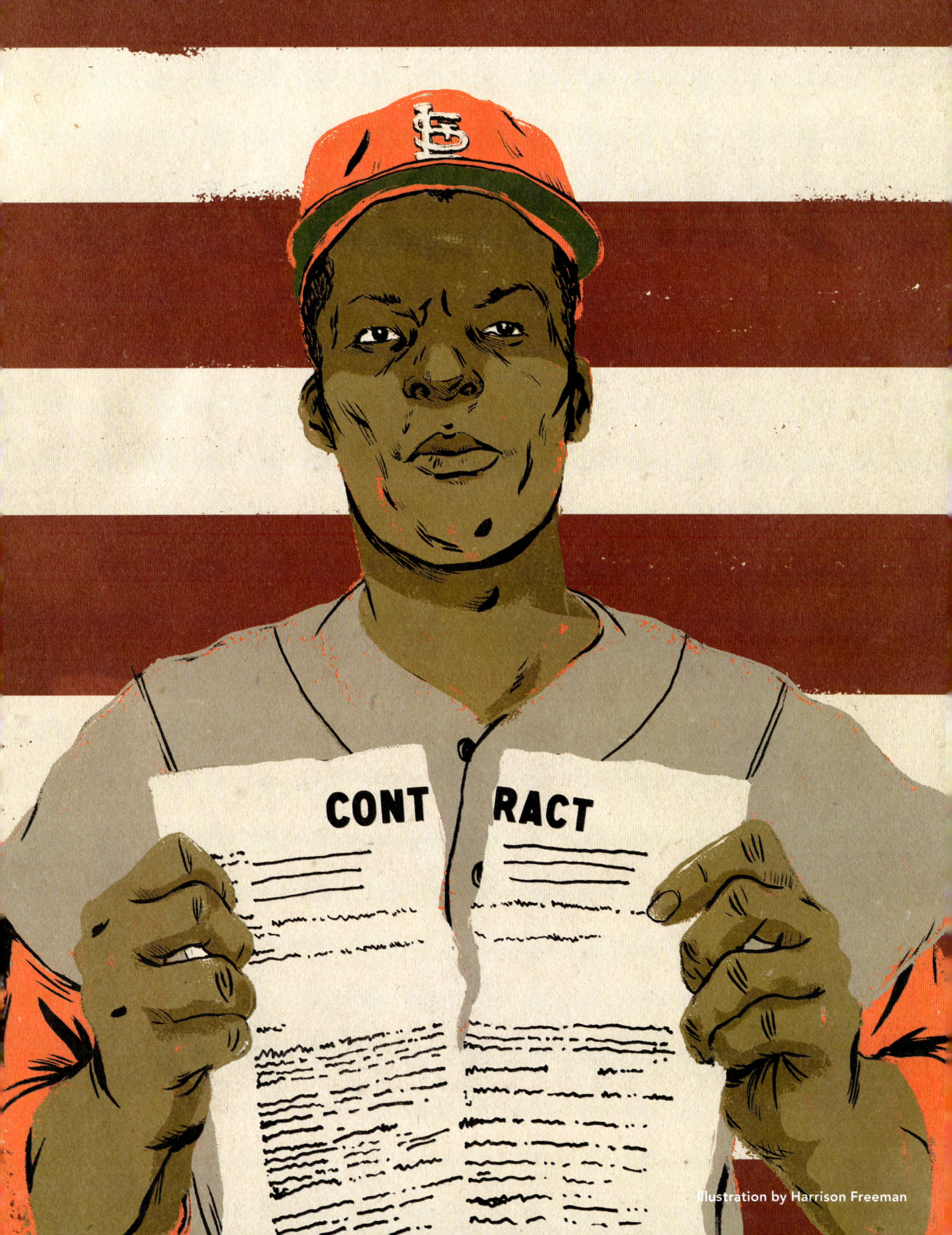

Illustration by Harrison Freeman

Daichi Suzuki

THE 15-METER RULE

The men's 100-meter backstroke final at the 1988 Summer Olympics was more submerged spectacle than Olympic sprint. Japanese swimmer Daichi Suzuki and American David Berkoff went head-to-head in a bizarre event where they swam nearly half the race underwater, forcing swimming to take a look at what really counts as a backstroke race.

The use of extended underwater swimming in backstroke was first pioneered by Jesse Vassallo in the late 1970s. Vassallo was a small swimmer at just 5-foot-9, and he began experimenting with longer underwater starts as a way to avoid the waves of bigger swimmers. Vassallo was a triple-medalist at the 1978 World Championships, but his swimming career was cut short when the United States boycotted the 1980 Olympic Games in Moscow during the Cold War. While Vassallo's underwater starts rarely extended beyond the first ten meters, Daichi Suzuki began to stretch his underwaters to the 25-meter mark. The submerged starts proved faster than traditional backstroke, and using the technique, Suzuki qualified for the 1984 Olympics. He failed to medal that year, but four years later, he was back in the pool for his game-changing duel with David Berkoff.

By 1988, Berkoff had taken the underwater tactic to a new level. He set American and world records by routinely pushing his submerged starts to 35 and 40 meters, almost the full length of an Olympic pool. Announcers coined the term "Berkoff Blastoff" for his powerful and extended underwaters.

On September 24, 1988, the stage was set for the 100-meter showdown. Suzuki in lane three. Berkoff in lane four. When the race began, all eight swimmers dove underwater. At 10 meters, the first racers surfaced. Berkoff and Suzuki were still underwater past 20 meters, then 30. Finally they surfaced around 35 meters. They reached the turn with Berkoff in the lead and then plunged back underwater for 10 more meters. When they resurfaced, Berkoff was still ahead with Suzuki closing in. They were tied with 20 meters to go. At the finish, Suzuki won gold by just 0.13 seconds.

Although the race was thrilling, the results of the 1988 100-meter backstroke go beyond gold, silver, and bronze. After the Olympics, FINA, swimming's governing body, banned underwater swimming in the backstroke beyond 10 meters, later extending it to 15. They stated safety concerns for swimmers willing to push their underwaters into dangerous territory without taking a breath. Vassallo, Suzuki, and Berkoff are remembered for their pioneering technique and the ripples they caused through their sport. All three men are honored in the International Swimming Hall of Fame.

David Berkoff

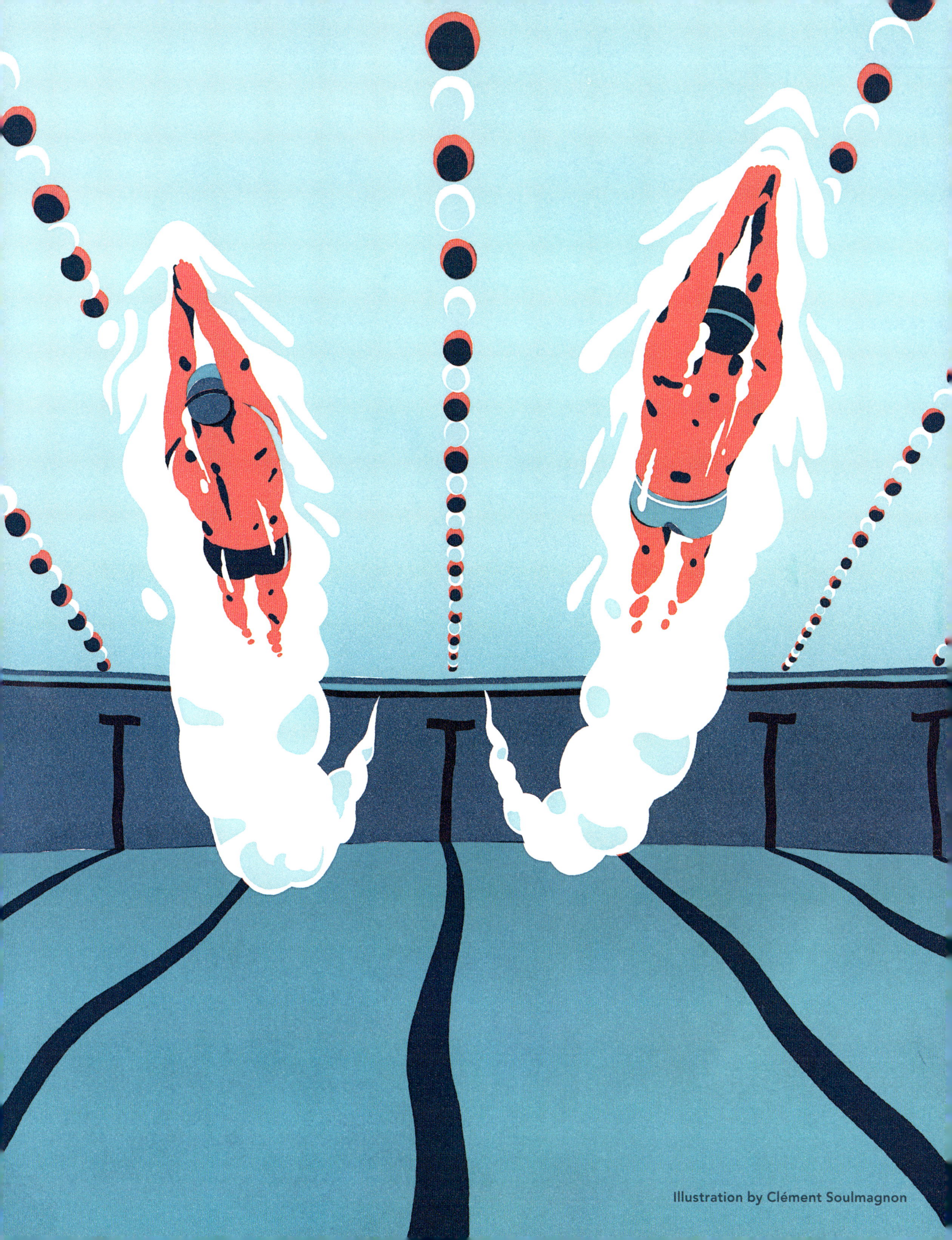

Illustration by Clément Soulmagnon

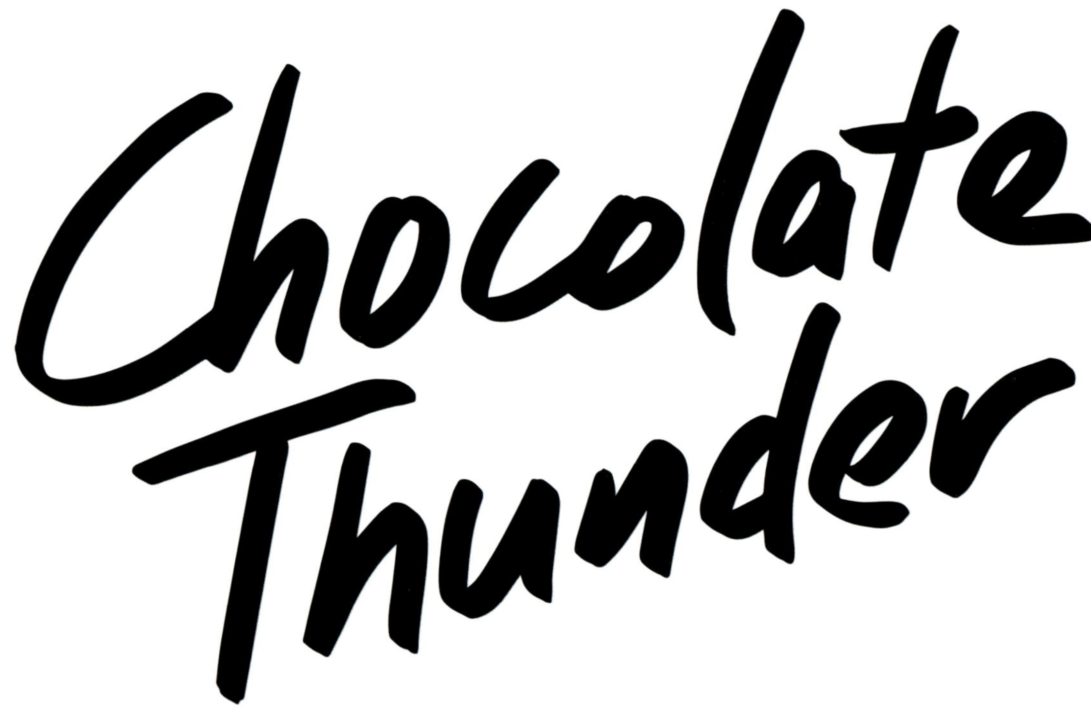

DARRYL DAWKINS

The Rim-Wrecker. The Spine-Chiller Supreme. The Go-Rilla. The In-Your-Face Disgrace. Darryl Dawkins named his best dunks like a rapper spouting lyrics. In a game on November 13, 1979, Dawkins threw down a monster jam over Kansas City Kings forward Bill Robinzine. The backboard exploded, raining shards of glass down on the players. Dawkins named that dunk The Chocolate-Thunder-Flying, Robinzine-Crying, Teeth-Shaking, Glass-Breaking, Rump-Roasting, Bun-Toasting, Wham-Bam, Glass-Breaker-I-Am-Jam. He later said, "It wasn't really a safe thing to do… but it was a Darryl Dawkins thing to do."

Dawkins was a character. A man-child who was the first player to go directly from high school to the NBA. He ate candy bars on the bench. He adorned himself with gold chains that read "Dr. Dunk" and "Sir Slam." Dawkins said, "I saw myself as a guy who enjoyed playing basketball, had a wild imagination, and was going to enjoy life." He was a gentle giant off the court, but on the court, he was a beast, blocking shots and throwing down dunks for the Philadelphia 76ers. His super slams inspired music legend Stevie Wonder to dub him "Chocolate Thunder." Word got around about Darryl's thunderous jams. Fans flocked to see him, and he always put on a show. The 6-foot-11, 250-pound Dawkins threw down dunks that punished the rim, shattering two backboards in the span of three weeks. NBA commissioner Larry O'Brien didn't like the trend. He quickly instituted a new rule stating any player hanging on the rim and shattering a backboard would be subject to a technical foul, fine, and possible suspension. Dawkins claimed innocence. "The commissioner is the police," Dawkins said. "He makes the rules; I've got to abide by them. It could be I just don't know my own strength. But seeing the scratches that the glass made in the floor, I think I'll cool it for a while."

Because of Dawkins, the NBA introduced breakaway rims in the early '80s, allowing the hoop to bend under the force of Double D. This innovation largely solved the problem of broken backboards until Shaquille O'Neal began tearing down the whole apparatus in the 1990s. For Dawkins, the game was always about having fun. He lived to entertain, and he'll always be remembered for bringing the thunder. "Darryl Dawkins is the father of power dunking," Shaquille O'Neal said. "I'm just one of his sons."

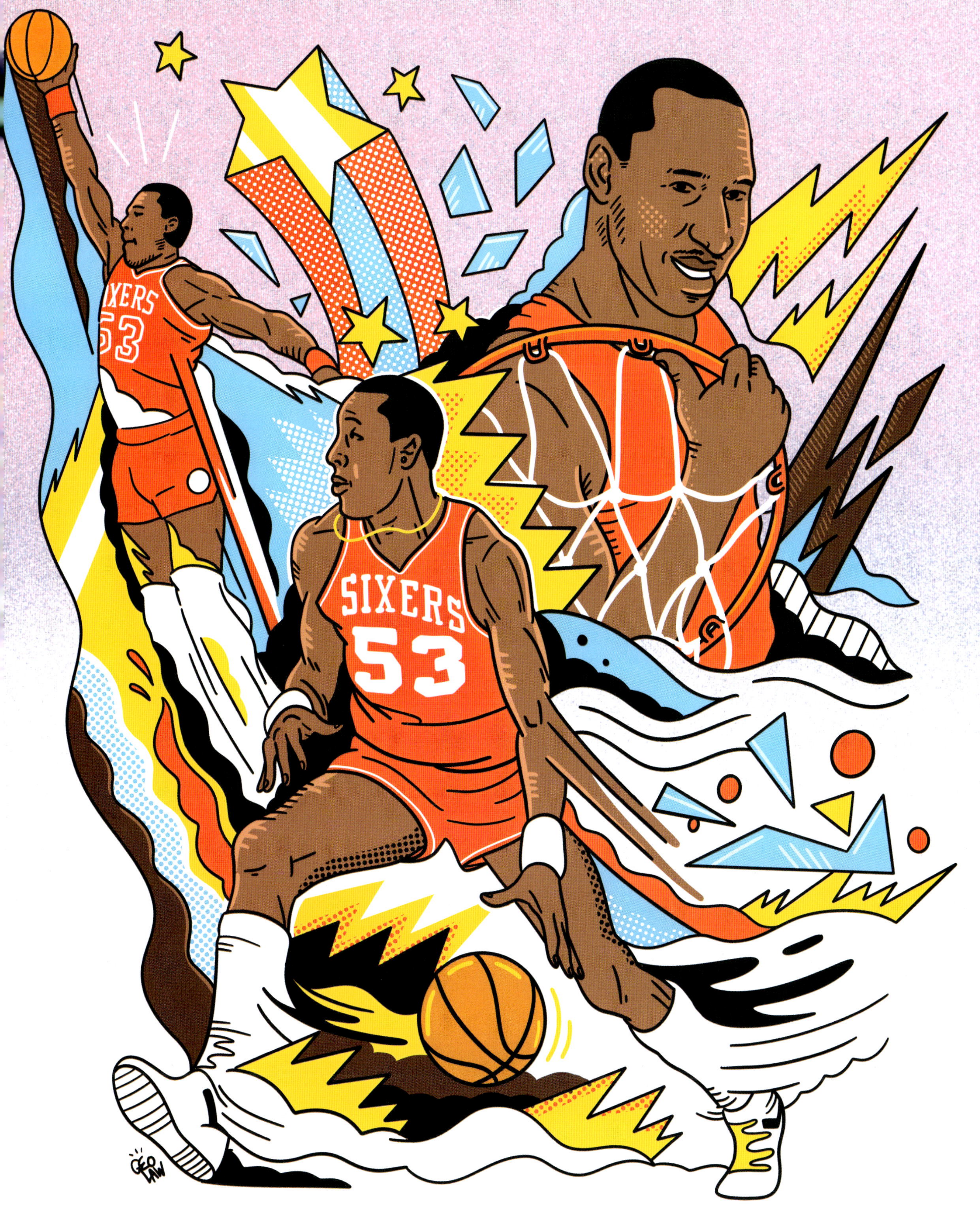

Illustration by Geo Law

"I FIGURE THEY GAVE YOU YOUR HANDS FOR SOMETHING."

—DAVE VOLZ

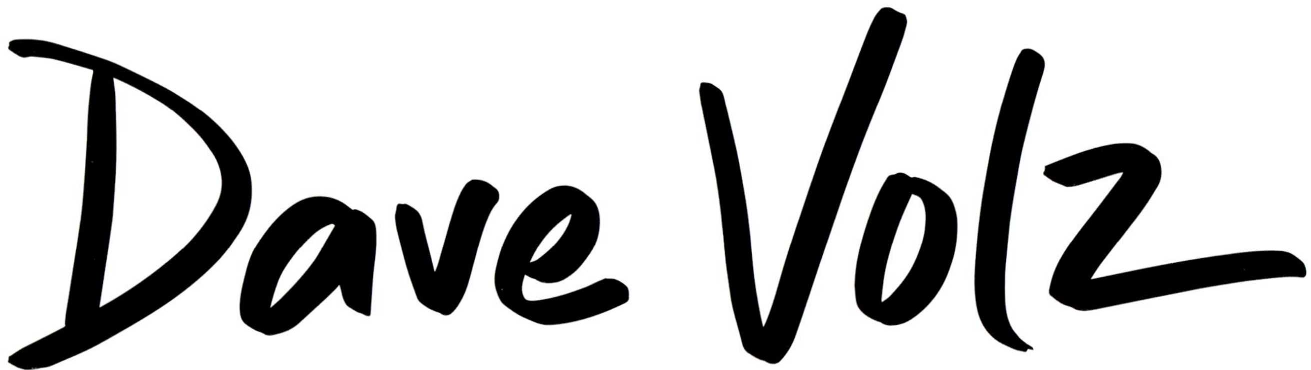

Dave Volz's approach to pole vaulting was a bit on the wild side. A friend and fellow vaulter said of him, "He's an animal.... He goes down that runway so hard he's almost out of control." Control wasn't something that concerned Dave, at least not while he was on the ground.

In the 1980s, Volz was one of the best pole vaulters in the world, in part because he pioneered a controversial mid-air move to help compensate for his chaotic run-up. If Dave bumped the crossbar while going over, he would reach out and steady it with his hands before falling into the pit. Volz said, "When I came over I hit the bar, so I tried to keep the bar balanced up there and it stayed up there pretty well. I seem to have a knack for it. I figure they gave you your hands for something." The unorthodox tactic required lightning-quick reflexes, and Dave studied film footage to perfect the skill. The new move became known as "Volzing."

Soon, more vaulters began adopting the technique, but others thought it was unfair. "Volzing ruins the event," complained Earl Bell, a fellow American vaulter. "If you miss, you should miss." Nonetheless, Volz continued to use the move. As a college freshman, Dave set the Big Ten conference indoor record with a vault of 18′2¼″. *Sports Illustrated* called it "the best American vault of the year." In 1982, Volz won both the indoor and outdoor Big Ten championships. That same year, he used Volzing to break the American record. *Track & Field News* called him "the best vaulter in the world." Coming off his record-setting year, Dave was primed to make an impact at the 1984 Olympics. Then disaster struck. Volz tripped over a misplaced bar during a competition warm-up and severed the nerves in his ankle. A series of injuries kept him from participating in the '84 and '88 Olympics. He finally got his chance in 1992, but his acrobatic move proved inconsequential. Volz placed fifth in the pole vault, out of the medals.

The controversial technique that Dave Volz pioneered is now banned by the International Amateur Athletic Federation, NCAA, and USA Track & Field. Had it not been for injury, Volzing may have played a more significant role in Olympic history. Regardless, Dave Volz carved his place in sports lore as the pole vaulter with the wild approach, the quick hands, and the record-setting move that still bears his name.

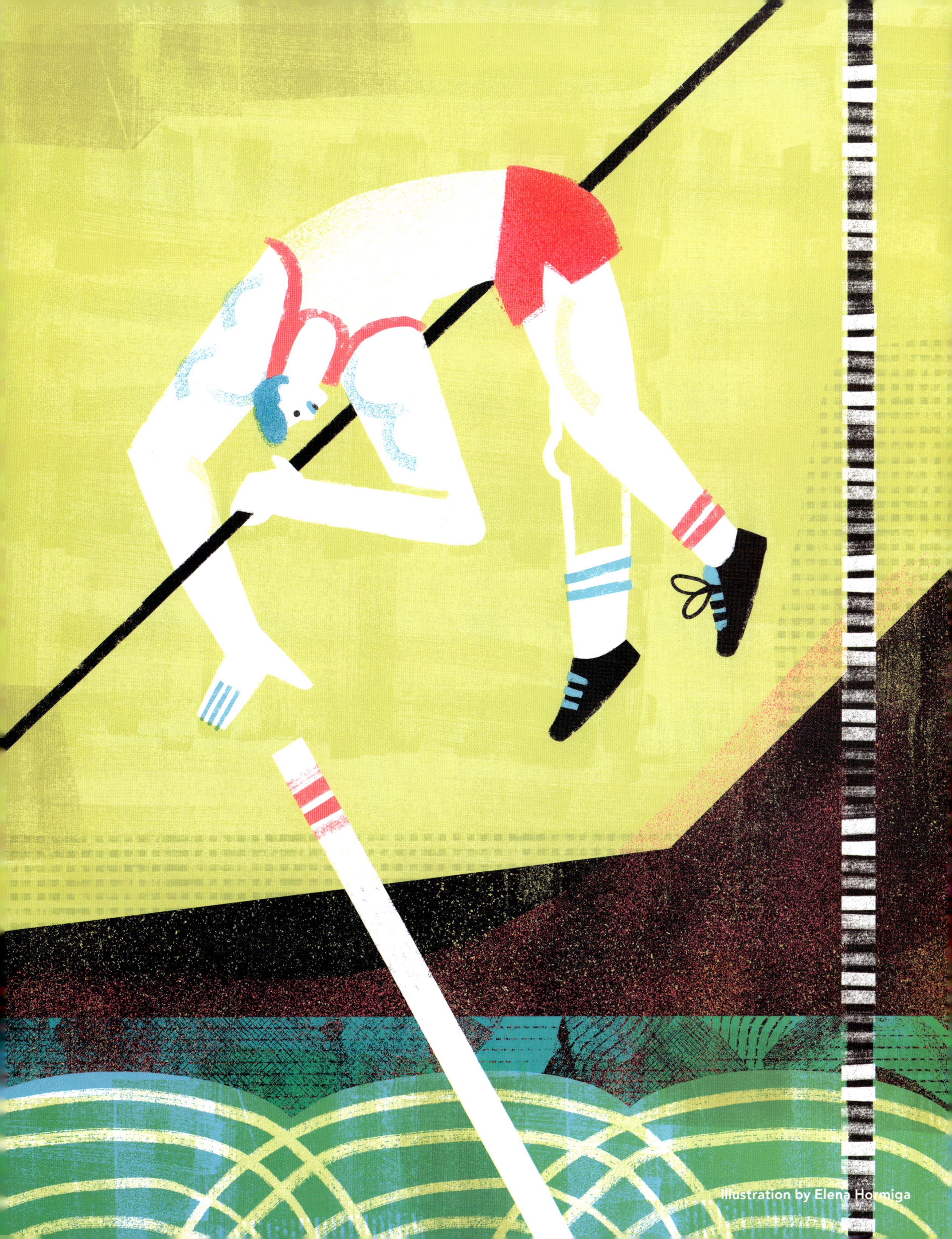
Illustration by Elena Hormiga

Fosbury Flop

DICK FOSBURY

When Dick Fosbury joined his high school track team in 1963, he dreamed of becoming a high jumper. But he couldn't even clear the 5-foot minimum height to qualify for most track meets. He tried the straddle method, the upright scissor, and the Western roll. Each technique saw jumpers leap over the bar forward, allowing them to land on their hands and feet. For the gangly Fosbury, the traditional methods required too much coordination. He said, "I knew I had to change my body position."

Soon Fosbury began experimenting with his own technique. He would leap over the bar backward, head-first, belly to the sky, and land on his back. His first attempts were far from graceful, some describing the method as an "airborne seizure." High jump pits of the 1960s were padded with sawdust and wood chips, hardly a soft landing for Fosbury's new approach. Ignoring splinters and injury, Dick practiced his technique and started seeing results. As his jumps grew higher, his landings became more dangerous. Thankfully, his high school became one of the first in the nation to adopt a foam landing zone.

During his junior year, Fosbury cleared 6'3", breaking his high school record. His senior year he jumped 6'5½", taking second place in the state. Despite his growing success, Fosbury had critics. One newspaper captioned a photo of him, "World's Laziest High Jumper," and another read, "Fosbury Flops Over Bar." This eventually led to the technique's name—the Fosbury Flop.

When Dick started college at Oregon State, his new coach, Berny Wagner, was skeptical of the flop and urged him to use the straddle method instead. Undeterred, Fosbury kept training with his unorthodox style. During his sophomore year, he used the flop to jump 6'10", breaking the school record. In 1968, Fosbury won both the indoor and outdoor NCAA championships and qualified for the Olympics in Mexico City. At the Olympics, Fosbury cleared 7'4¼", winning gold and setting Olympic and US records. He said, "I was told over and over again that I would never be successful, that I was not going to be competitive and the technique was simply not going to work. All I could do was shrug and say, 'We'll just have to see.'" At the next Olympics in 1972, 28 of the 40 high jumpers used Fosbury's method. It has become the most widely used technique in high jump, and every world-record holder since 1980 has floated over the bar using the Fosbury Flop.

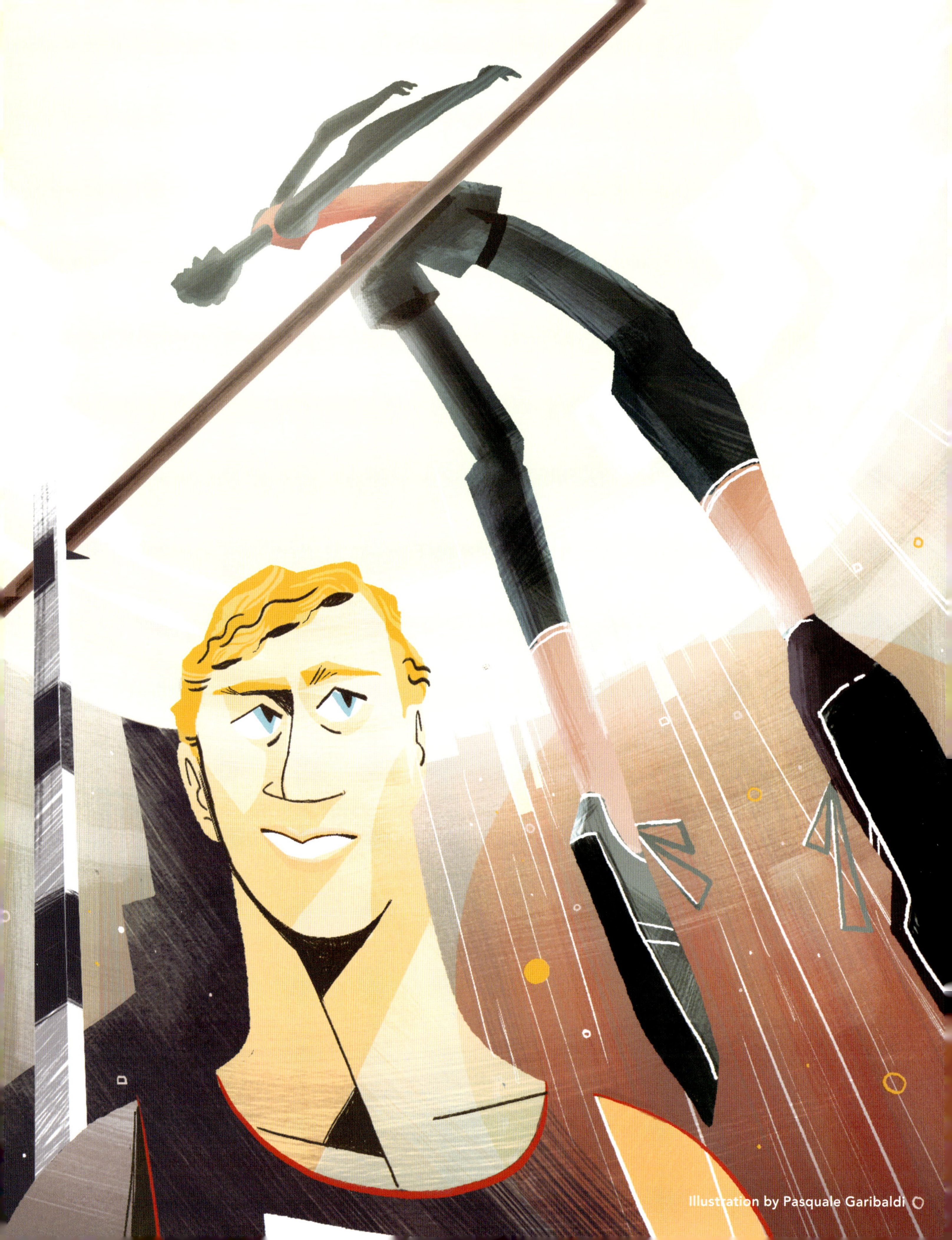
Illustration by Pasquale Garibaldi

Disgrace of Gijón

1982 WORLD CUP

There weren't many expectations for Algeria when they made their World Cup debut in 1982. After all, an African team had never beaten a European squad, and their first match was against West Germany, the current European champions. The Germans were confident they'd win, saying, "We will dedicate our seventh goal to our wives, and our eighth to our dogs." On June 16, 1982, the two teams met, and Algeria embarrassed West Germany, winning 2-1. The match was described as "one of the biggest shocks in World Cup history."

Algeria lost their next match to Austria, then defeated Chile 3-2. Despite their incredible start, the African team was on the cusp of elimination. Their fate would be determined by a match between Austria and West Germany, the team they had humiliated a week earlier. Based on the World Cup point system, Algeria would advance if Austria beat West Germany or the Germans beat Austria by three or more goals. But if the Germans won 1-0 or 2-0, both Austria and West Germany would move forward, and the Algerians would be sent home.

On June 25, the deciding match kicked off in Gijón, Spain. In the 10th minute, Horst Hrubesch scored, putting West Germany up 1-0. After the early goal, the action subsided. Neither team attacked, and shots were few and far between. The second half saw only three shots in total, none of which were on target. Both sides seemed content to stay at 1-0. The crowd was disgusted. Algerian fans waved money, yelling, "It's a fix!" German commentator Eberhard Stanjek said, "What's happening here is disgraceful and has nothing to do with football," while Austrian TV commentator Robert Seeger told viewers to turn off their televisions. The match ended with West Germany winning 1-0. Both European squads advanced, and Algeria was eliminated.

The Algerian team immediately filed a complaint, claiming the two teams conspired together. FIFA investigated, and after less than four hours determined that there was no proof of tampering. Hermann Neuberger, a FIFA vice-president, said, "There are no FIFA rules which say teams cannot play as they please." Neuberger was also the president of the West German Soccer Federation. At the next World Cup in 1986, FIFA modified its rules so the final two games in any group would be played simultaneously, eliminating predetermined outcomes. Algerian player Lakhdar Belloumi said, "Our performances forced FIFA to make that change, and that was even better than a victory. It meant that Algeria left an indelible mark on football history."

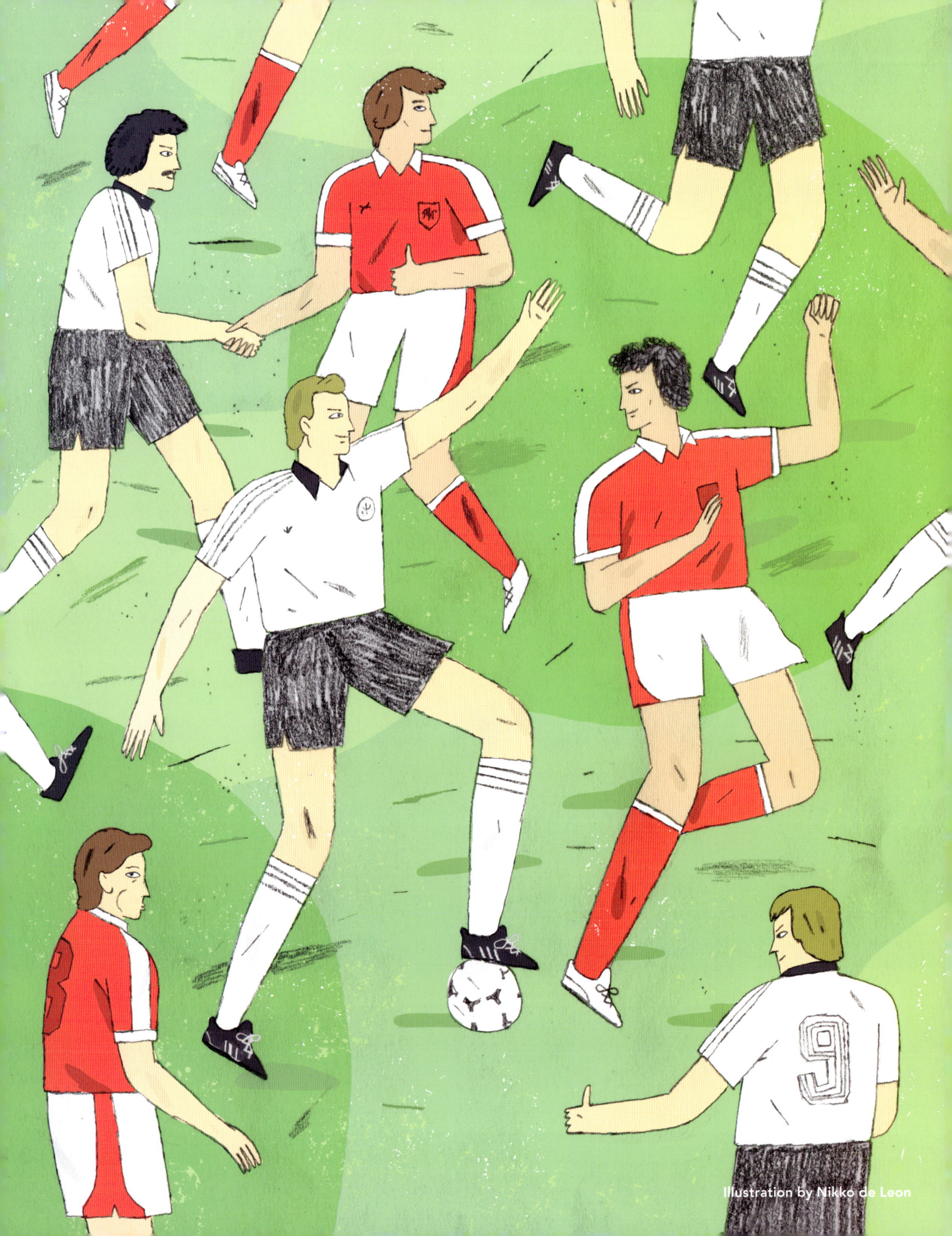

Illustration by Nikko de Leon

Doug Allison

THE BASEBALL MITT

A bat, a ball, and a mitt. The most iconic items in baseball. But that wasn't always the case. During baseball's early years, players didn't wear gloves. Their hands took a beating, suffering broken bones, dislocated joints, and bloodied fingers. Catchers and first basemen often needed days off to recover. "For a catcher to appear in 100 games in a season was considered an incredible marvel of endurance," noted baseball glove historian Denny Esken. Players thought it was unmanly to wear gloves, and those who did were ridiculed by fans and opponents.

Cincinnati Red Stockings catcher Doug Allison was among the first to wear a glove. In the late 1860s, most catchers stood 25 feet behind the batter, scooping up pitches barehanded after one or two bounces. Allison innovated the position by standing immediately behind the hitter to discourage baserunners from stealing home. "It took immense courage to get up behind the batter," said MLB historian John Thorn. Catching pitches at a closer range made the job even more dangerous, and Allison was frequently hurt. For a game on June 28, 1870, he reluctantly donned a glove to protect an injured hand. Baseball historian Noah Liberman wrote that Allison "was razzed by opposing players and fans." The glove disappeared from the game for the next five years.

In 1875, first baseman Charlie Waitt brought the glove back, though he had hoped to go unnoticed by wearing a flesh-colored mitt. Fans weren't fooled, and they taunted him for being weak. A.G. Spalding, a popular pitcher at the time, curiously asked Charlie about the glove. Waitt confessed he was ashamed to wear it, but he somehow had to save his injured hand. Spalding saw a lucrative opportunity and started a sporting-goods company the next year, offering baseball gloves as one of his first products. In a brilliant marketing stroke, Spalding boldly wore a black glove onto the field during an 1877 game. His stellar reputation thwarted any criticism, and after Spalding's stunt, the players and the public began to accept the mitt.

By 1895, gloves were so commonplace that the first official rules were created to standardize their size. Inventors began patenting designs for every position and use. What was once considered an embarrassing accessory is now proudly endorsed by the game's top players. Superstar signatures are burned into the leather, and the best fielders win Gold Glove Awards. The baseball mitt has become an essential part of the game and an enduring icon of America's favorite pastime.

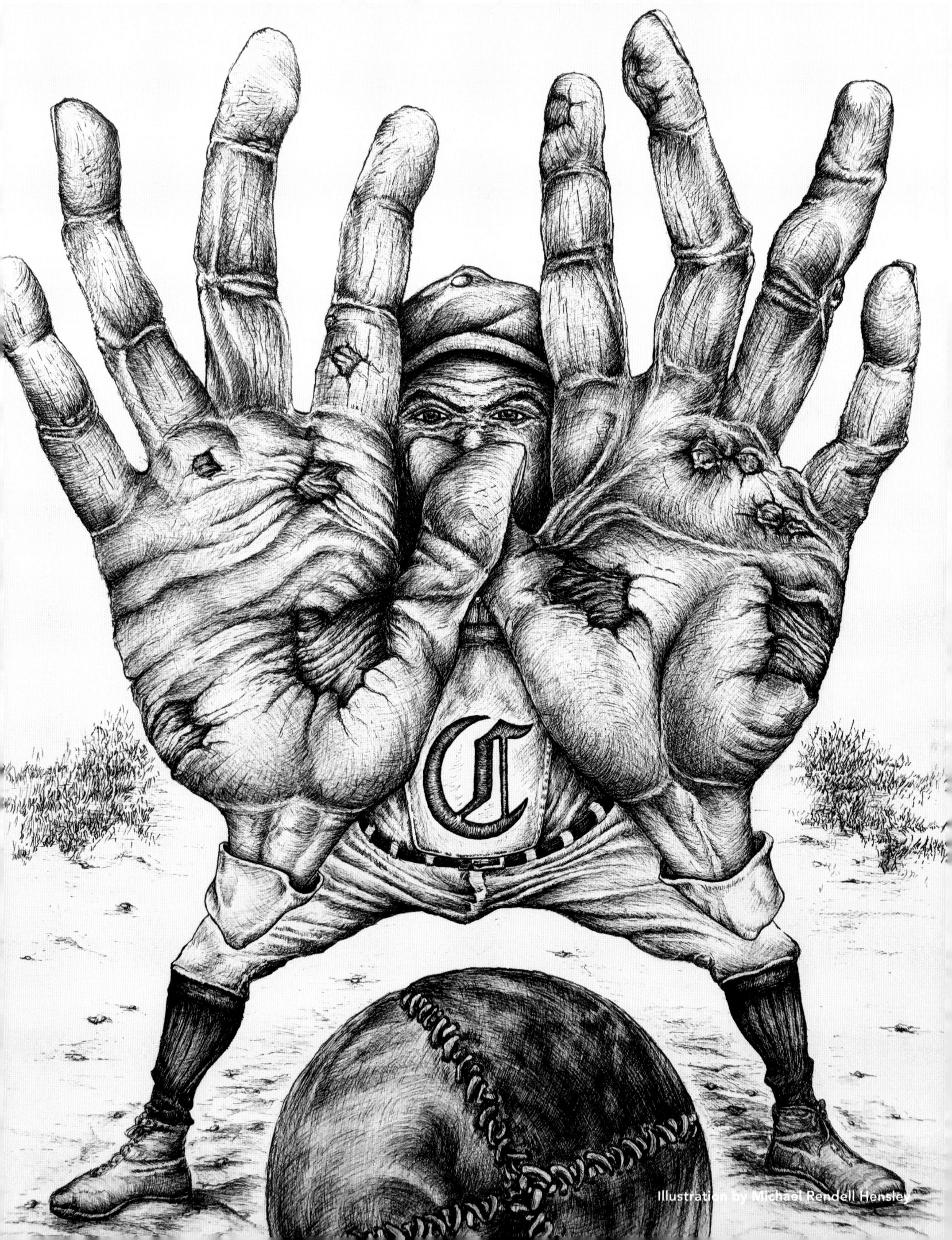
Illustration by Michael Rendell Hensley

Ed Walsh

There is perhaps no pitch more vile, disgusting, and devious than the spitball. Spitter. Mud ball. Shine ball. Grease ball. The nefarious pitch goes by many names, and for batters in the early 1900s, it was a devil to hit. Anything a pitcher could do to alter the ball was fair game. Spitting was common, but some pitchers rubbed the ball with mud to make it harder to see, sanded parts of the leather with emery cloth, or even coated the ball with Vaseline. The doctored pitch tumbled through the air with the speed of a fastball and the movement of a knuckleball.

While many early pitchers experimented with some version of the spitball, Ed Walsh was the man to popularize it. "Big Ed Walsh. Great big, strong, good-looking fellow.... He threw a spitball. I think that ball disintegrated on the way to the plate," said Hall of Fame outfielder Sam Crawford. "I swear, when it went past the plate it was just the spit went by." Walsh's spitball was considered the best in baseball. He tried to mask the pitch, going to his mouth before every throw, even on non-spitters. According to baseball author Alfred Henry Spink, when Walsh did throw the spitter, he wet a spot about an inch big between the seams of the ball. He clenched his thumb tightly on the opposite seam and swung his arm straight overhead with terrific force. Spink wrote, "At times it will dart two feet down and out, depending on the way his arm is swung." The spitter worked for Walsh. He still holds the major league record for lowest career ERA at 1.82 and is one of only two pitchers since 1900 to win more than 40 games in a season. He's also a Hall of Famer.

Major League Baseball outlawed the spitball in 1920, with the exception of a few pitchers who were still allowed to throw it until they retired. Rumors swirled as to why the pitch was banned. The dirt and tobacco-stained spitballs were hard to see, and some thought they posed a safety risk. Others believed it had more to do with money. In his autobiography, baseball legend Ty Cobb wrote that "freak pitches" were outlawed when the owners "greedily sold out to home runs." Whatever the reason, by 1921, runs per game had increased by 30%, and teams were hitting more than three times as many home runs as they had in 1918. The soggy dead-ball era of baseball was over, and the game entered a new age of "live-ball."

> "BIG ED WALSH... HE THREW A SPITBALL... I SWEAR, WHEN IT WENT PAST THE PLATE IT WAS JUST THE SPIT WENT BY."
>
> —SAM CRAWFORD, HALL OF FAME OUTFIELDER

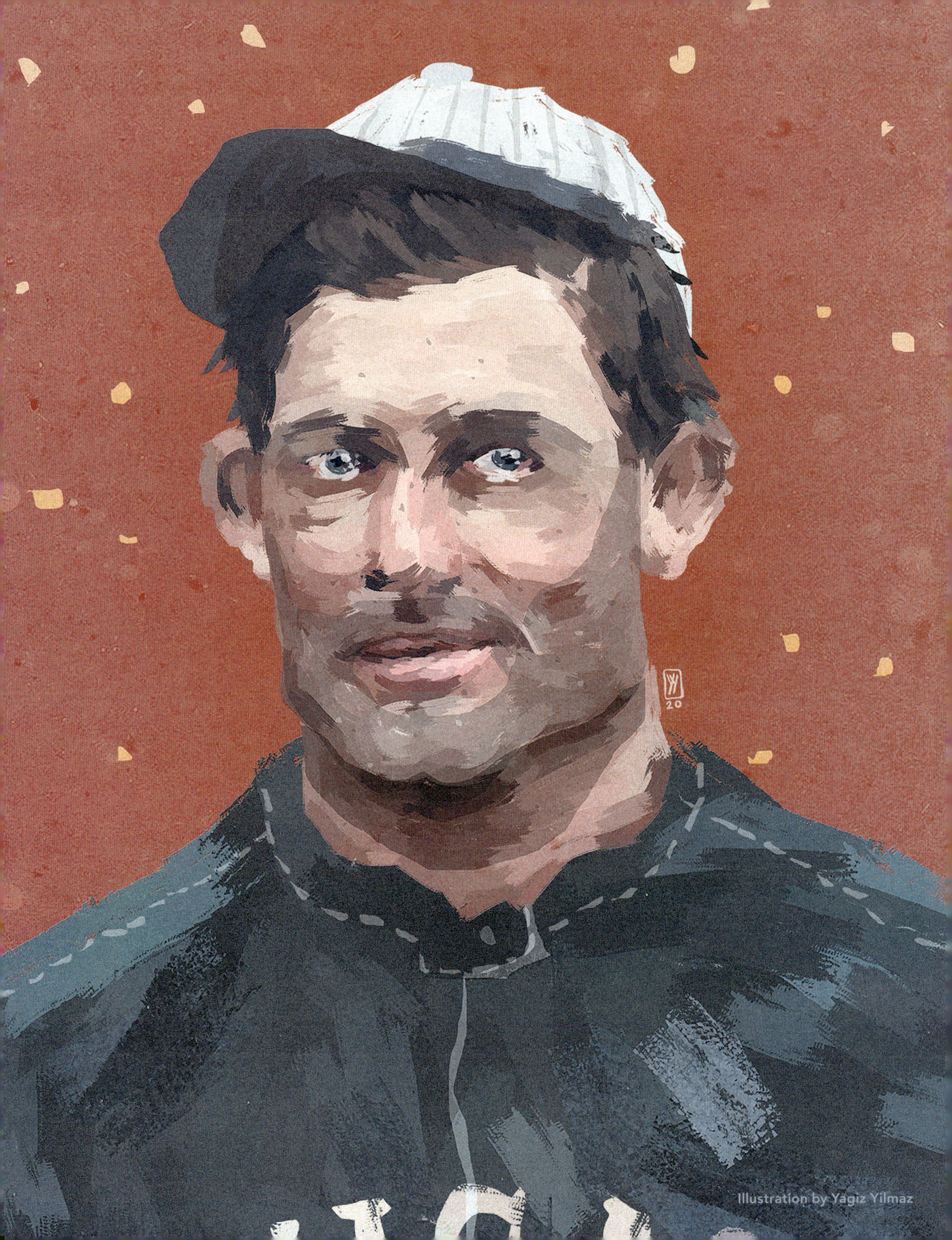
Illustration by Yagiz Yilmaz

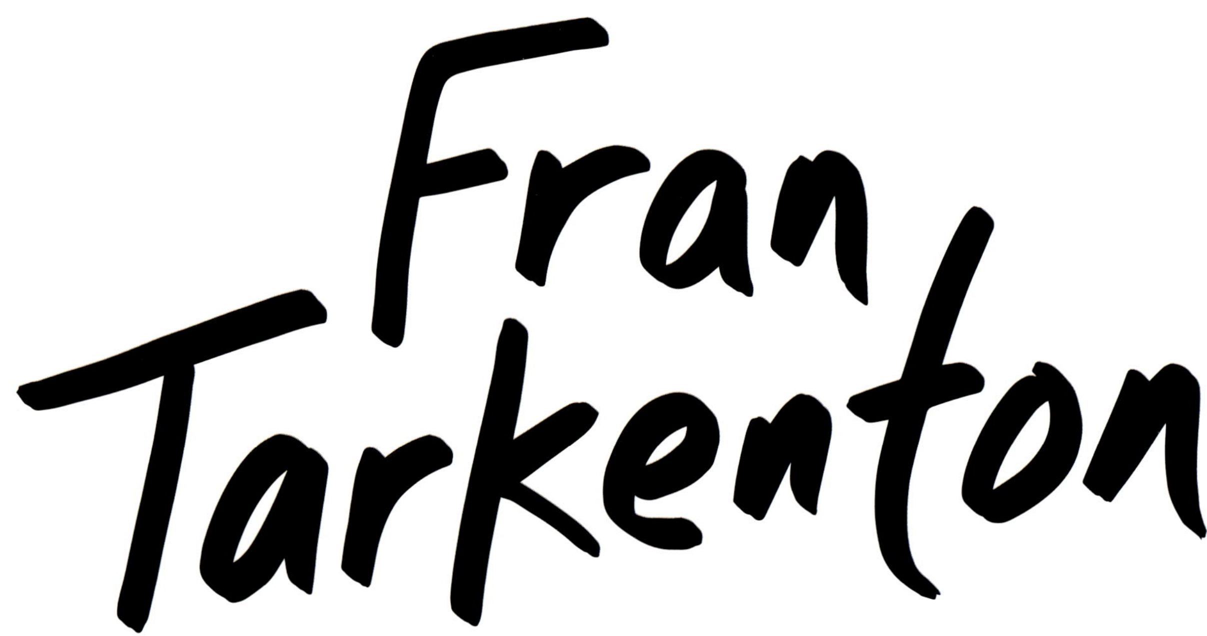

THE DUAL-THREAT QUARTERBACK

Dual-threat quarterbacks—players who could devastate defenses with their passing and running ability—have a complicated history in the NFL. Their roots trace back to scrambling signal callers who used their athleticism to make defenses miss. Tobin Rote is considered by many to be the first running passer. In 1956, he was the NFL leader in quarterback rushing yards, quarterback rushing touchdowns, passing yards, and passing touchdowns. Despite his individual achievements, Rote was on a series of mediocre teams and failed to prove that a running quarterback could consistently win in the NFL. That task fell to "Frantic" Fran Tarkenton.

Tarkenton wrote, "When I began my NFL career in 1961, I was a freak. The reason was simple: I played quarterback and I ran. There were no designed runs in our playbook, but I would scramble out of the pocket when a play broke down.... It was not a skill set that was embraced. Plenty of people mocked it, and the rest wrote it off." Fran played when statue quarterbacks dominated the game. These drop-back passers stood in the pocket, and if there were no receivers open, they inevitably took a sack. Tarkenton was different. He was fast and elusive. He used his speed to escape defenders and extend plays. Nicknamed the "Mad Scrambler," Fran won games through the air and on the ground. When he retired after 18 seasons, he was the NFL leader in career passing yards, career passing touchdowns, career quarterback rushing yards, and wins by a quarterback. He is also the only quarterback to score a rushing touchdown in 15 different seasons.

Tarkenton proved that a running quarterback could win. But even after his retirement in 1978, it would take another few decades for the NFL to warm to the idea. Racial undertones clouded the adoption of running passers. With a few exceptions, dual-threat quarterbacks were viewed as Black quarterbacks, and many owners and coaches didn't believe a Black player could run the offense. Gradually, past prejudices began to fade away, and the league saw more Black signal callers under center. In the 2000s, the NFL finally embraced running quarterbacks such as Michael Vick, Russell Wilson, and Cam Newton. This time, it was the defenses left scrambling to adapt. The cat-and-mouse game between offense and defense will continue to evolve, but for now, dual-threat quarterbacks have found a place on the field, in part because of the fleet feet of "Frantic" Fran.

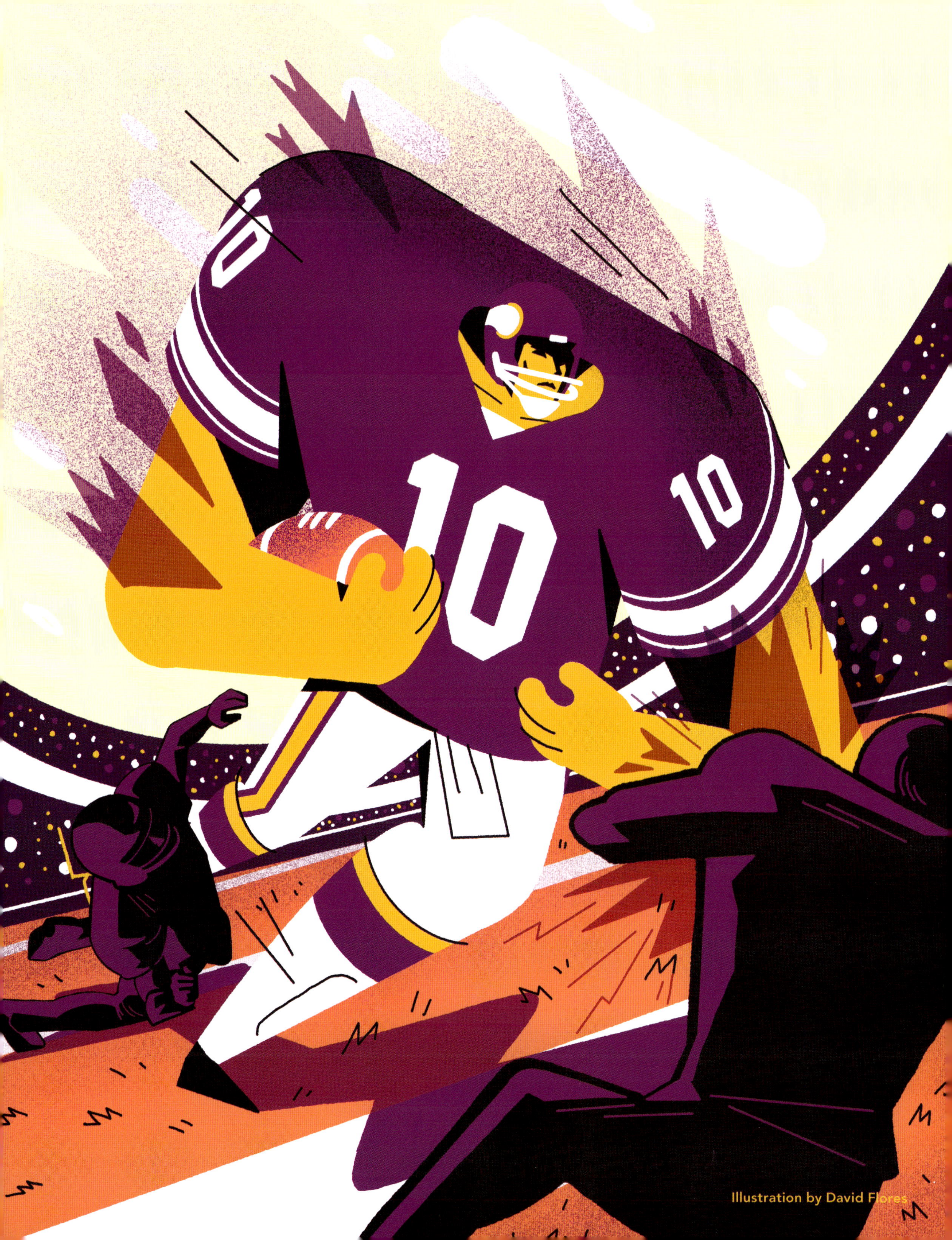

Illustration by David Flores

George Mikan

THE BIG MAN

"George Mikan truly revolutionized the game," said NBA commissioner David Stern. "We may never see one man impact the game of basketball as he did." Mikan's journey through basketball got off to a rocky start. In the 1940s, coaches thought tall players like 6-foot-10 Mikan were too uncoordinated to play. During a tryout for Notre Dame, coach George Keogan said, "He's too awkward and he wears glasses." Mikan recalled, "No matter where a tall guy went in those days, there was always someone to tell him he couldn't do something." But DePaul coach Ray Meyer saw a diamond in the rough. He trained Mikan using boxing and dance to improve his footwork. He had him practice hundreds of hook shots, from the left and the right, still known today as "Mikan drills." Meyer said, "I'm ashamed of how hard I worked him."

The work paid off. Mikan was a three-time All-American at DePaul, and after college, he joined the National Basketball League. In 1949, the NBL merged with another league to form the NBA, and Mikan quickly became its biggest star. He led the league in scoring and rebounding, winning five of the first six championships with the Minneapolis Lakers. He was so popular that during one game against New York, the marquee at Madison Square Garden read, "Geo Mikan vs. Knicks." Mikan's height and athleticism broke the game of basketball, forcing the rules to change. The NCAA created a goaltending rule to stop him from snatching shots out of the air. The NBA doubled the width of the lane to keep him from posting under the basket. Mikan still dominated. In a 1950 game, the Fort Wayne Pistons tried playing "keep-away" from Mikan, holding and dribbling the ball instead of shooting. This led to the lowest-scoring NBA game of all time and the introduction of the shot clock. The Pistons beat the Lakers 19-18. Mikan had 15 of the Lakers' 18 points.

Mikan was the NBA's first "big man" and a true ambassador of the sport. He said, "Back in those old days, I'd arrive by train or plane a day or two ahead of the team to promote the game." Mikan was instrumental in growing the NBA into what it is today. He said, "I never minded any of the extra obligations. You know, when you think about it, it was pretty good stuff for the big kid with the glasses who nobody thought would be able to play. Now all these years later, I'm just happy to have left my mark."

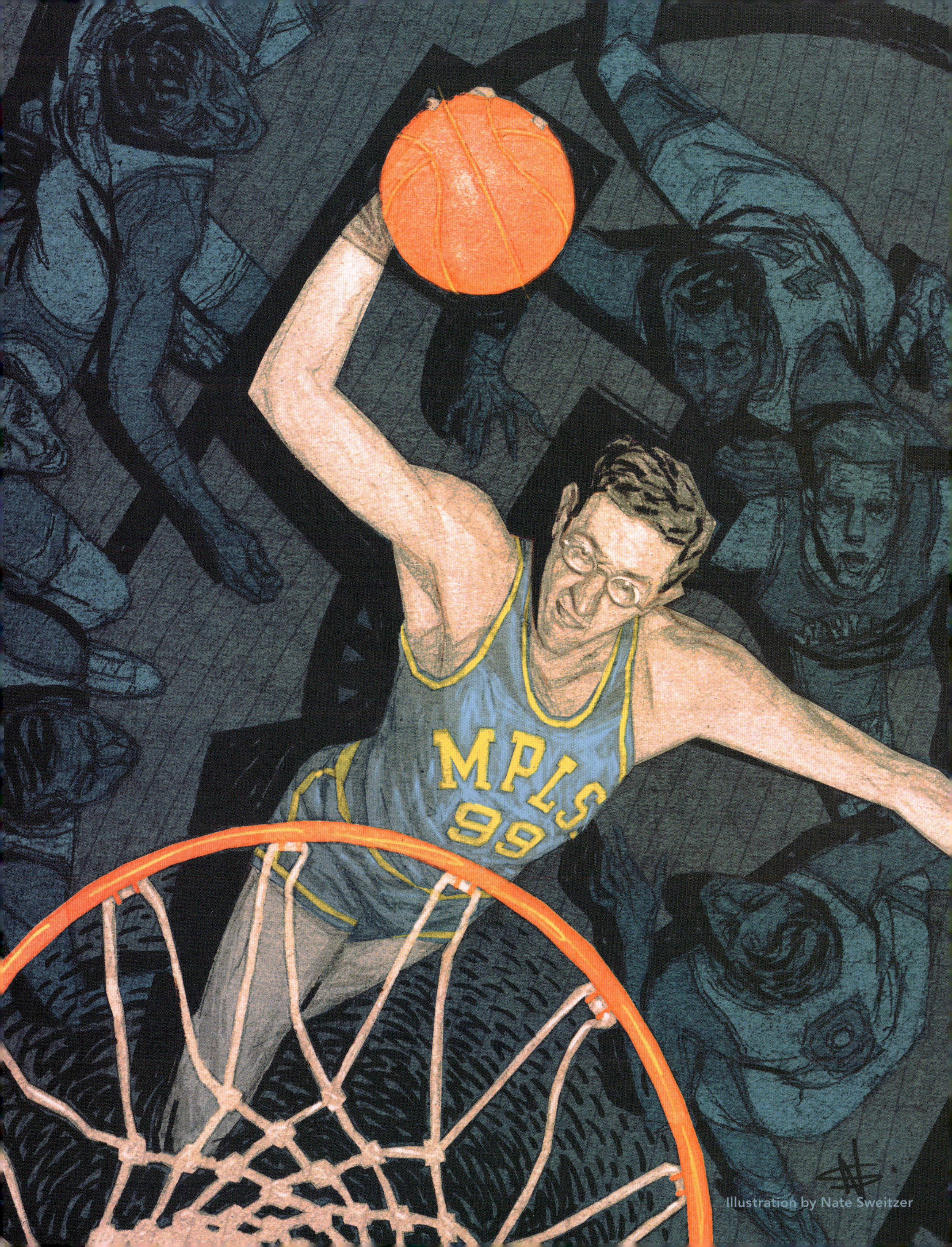

Illustration by Nate Sweitzer

"WITH THE TEAR-AWAYS, THEY DIDN'T GET ME RIGHT, THEY'D END UP WITH JUST A JERSEY IN THEIR HAND AND I'D BE GONE."

—GREG PRUITT

Greg Pruitt

Greg Pruitt knew how to tear through a defense. "My style was elusive," he said. The shifty running back cut and slashed his way to three consecutive 1,000-yard seasons for the Cleveland Browns in the 1970s. Defenders had a hard time tackling Pruitt, in part, because of his ingenious use of tear-away jerseys. "Nobody could ever get a squared-up, dead, knockout blow on me but they were always reaching and grabbing because of my size. They could actually tackle me that way. With the tear-aways, they didn't get me right, they'd end up with just a jersey in their hand and I'd be gone."

Tear-away jerseys had been used for years before, but Pruitt perfected the practice. When running, he bounced and dodged through the defense, leaving opponents with handfuls of cotton. "For it to be effective, you couldn't wear anything under it, or they'd just grab that shirt," he said. Once his jersey was ripped to shreds, he ran to the sideline, where the equipment manager had another shirt ready. He tore off the old shirt and slid into a fresh jersey. Pruitt was back in the huddle without missing a snap. He compared the process to a NASCAR pit stop, sometimes going through four or five jerseys a game. There was an art to the shirt's construction. Kent Stephens, a curator at the College Football Hall of Fame, said, "The material they are made out of is very difficult to explain. They are cotton, and the best way to explain them is imagining an old, worn out t-shirt. The two we have are quite brittle, and I worry every time we display them that that's going to be the end of them."

The NFL outlawed tear-away jerseys in 1979 in what's commonly referred to as the "Greg Pruitt Rule." The NCAA followed suit in 1982. Despite his success with the tear-away, Pruitt was relieved by the ban. "I want them to know I was getting a lot of yards before the tear-away," he said. "It's not like magic. You've got to do something in the jersey." Pruitt added that he also didn't miss hurrying to the sidelines and changing shirts in Cleveland's icy wind. Pruitt played for five more seasons, but he was never able to replicate the success he found while wearing tear-aways. He is fifth on the Browns all-time rushing list, and his eponymous rule has cemented his legacy in the history of football—something nobody can rip away from him.

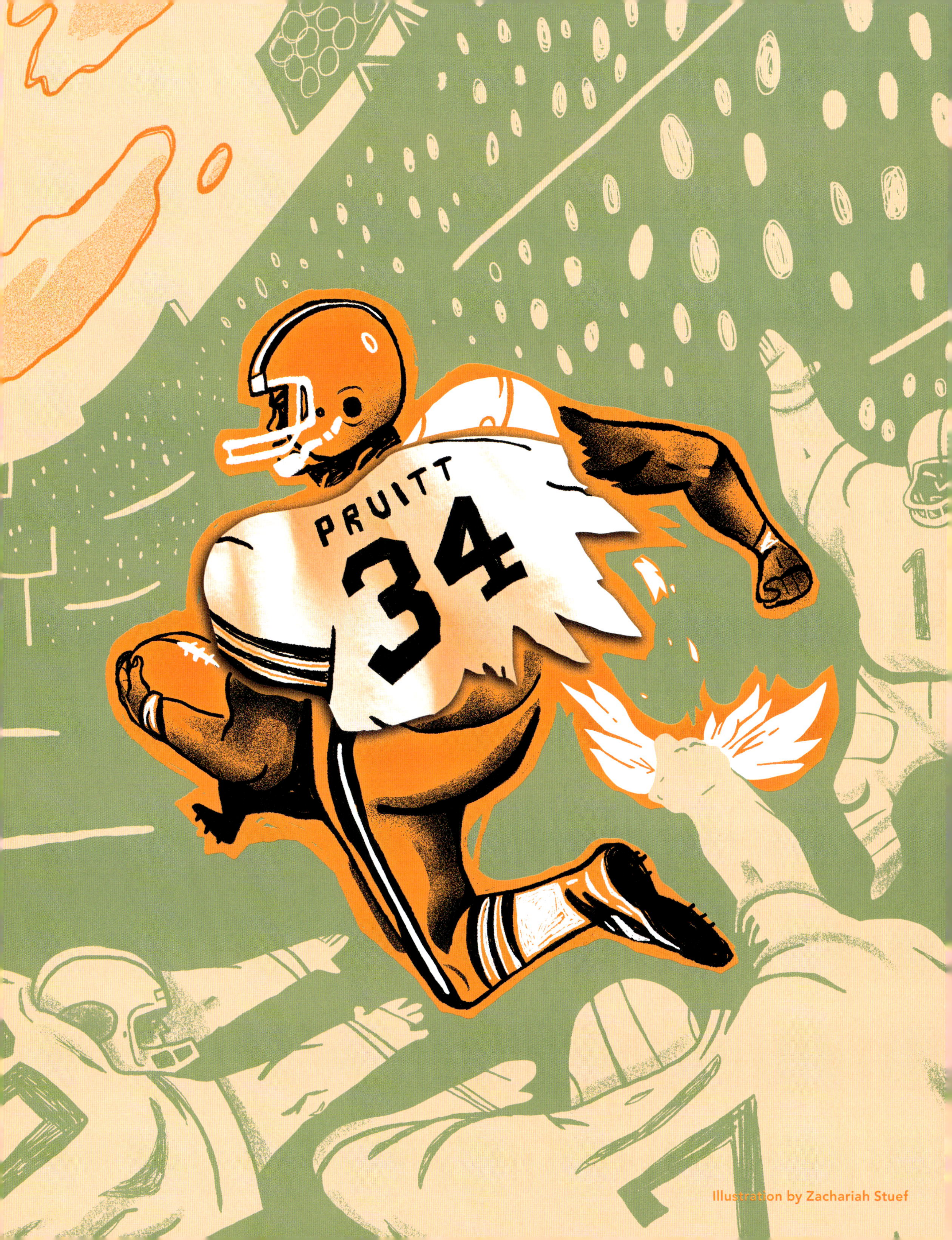

Illustration by Zachariah Stuef

Homer Jones

THE TOUCHDOWN SPIKE

On October 17, 1965, Homer Jones was starting in his first NFL game for the New York Giants. Jones was a lightning-fast receiver, and it didn't take long for him to make an impact on the field. In the second quarter, Homer caught a pass from quarterback Earl Morrall and took off, 89 yards for his first touchdown. He had seen teammates Alex Webster and Frank Gifford toss the football into the stands after scoring, so Homer planned to do the same. But before he did, he remembered NFL commissioner Pete Rozelle had recently banned tossing the ball to fans, punishable by a $500 fine.

"I was fixing to throw it into the grandstand," Jones recalled. "But just as I was raising my arm, the reality snapped into my head. Mr. Rozelle would have fined me. That was a lot of money in those days. So I just threw the ball down into the end zone, into the grass. Folks got excited, and I did it for the rest of my career."

Homer later referred to the move as a "spike," inventing football's most iconic touchdown celebration. Jones was an electrifying player with a knack for making big plays with his blistering speed. He reached the end zone 38 times in his career, and each one ended with a touchdown spike. Jones changed the culture of the NFL and set off a celebration chain reaction that continues to this day. Some players made celebrations part of their persona, like the Funky Chicken, the Ickey Shuffle, and the Gronk Spike. Some teams made it a tradition, like the Lambeau Leap and the Mile High Salute. And then players such as Terrell Owens and Chad "Ochocinco" Johnson took their outlandish celebrations to a new level. After a touchdown in 2002, Owens pulled a marker from his sock and autographed the football in front of cameras before tossing it into the stands. The NFL thought the party was getting out of hand, and in 2006 it started penalizing players for "excessive celebration." Fans began referring to the league by a new NFL, the "No Fun League."

In 2017, the NFL relaxed its restrictions on celebrations, bringing some of the fun back to the game. Ironically, it was a league ban in 1965 that started the celebration craze. Because of a $500 fine, Homer Jones thought twice about tossing the ball to fans, spiked it into the ground, and pioneered a move that would become as iconic as the game itself.

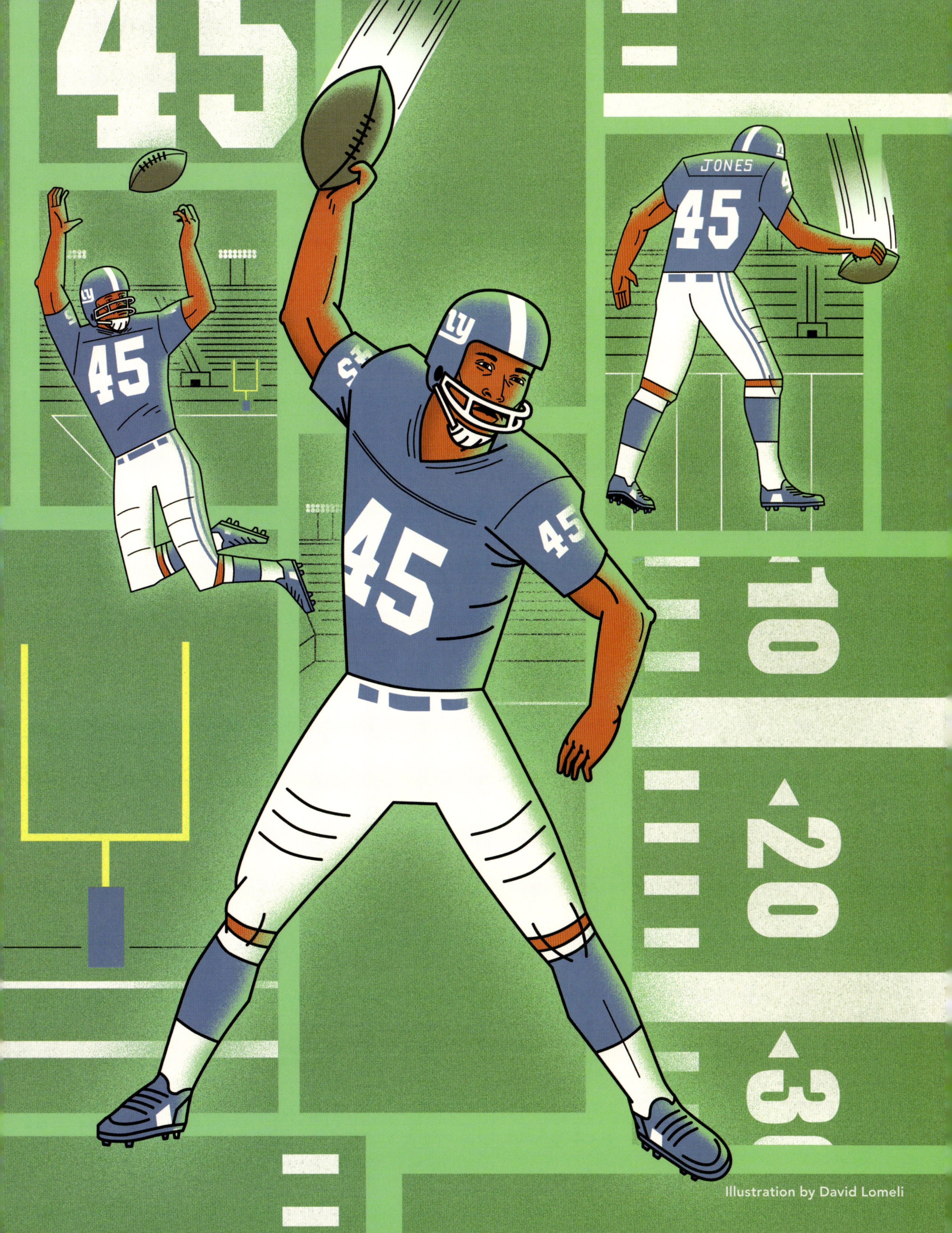

Illustration by David Lomeli

Jackie Robinson

On April 15, 1947, Jackie Robinson took to the field for the Brooklyn Dodgers, making history as the first African American player in Major League Baseball. Dodgers owner Branch Rickey had been looking to integrate the league and thought Robinson was the "right man" to break the color barrier. He was college-educated, a military officer, and a star athlete at UCLA. But he was also a hothead, especially when confronted with racism. Branch knew Jackie would face constant racial abuse, and he worried that his temper would set back their goal of integration. Before agreeing to a contract, Rickey challenged Robinson, asking if he had the guts to "not fight back." Jackie promised there would be "no incident" and signed with the Dodgers.

During his rookie year, Jackie endured taunts and slurs. Pitchers aimed for his head. "I don't know any other ball players who could have done what he did," said Dodgers teammate Pee Wee Reese. "To be able to hit with everybody yelling at him... to do what he did has got to be the most tremendous thing I've ever seen in sports." On the surface, Jackie kept his emotions in check, but underneath he seethed, saying, "Plenty of times I wanted to haul off when somebody insulted me for the color of my skin, but I had to hold to myself. I knew I was kind of an experiment. The whole thing was bigger than me." Robinson's outstanding play began to turn the crowds. In 1947, he was baseball's first Rookie of the Year, helping the Dodgers reach the World Series. By the end of the year, a national popularity poll placed him second behind only singer Bing Crosby. Branch and Jackie's experiment was working, and in 1949 they both agreed it was time to start fighting back. Rickey told Robinson, "You can be yourself now."

Robinson became a powerful voice in the battle against racism. He publicly criticized teams that wouldn't hire Black players. He fought segregation, demanding restaurants and hotels treat Black and White players equally. He testified before the US Congress on discrimination, and he served on the board of the NAACP for a decade. Martin Luther King Jr. said of Robinson, "He was a sit-inner before sit-ins, a freedom rider before freedom rides." Jackie Robinson was a champion on and off the field. He was an inspiration to generations of oppressed people, fighting for equality. Robinson said, "There's not an American in this country free until every one of us is free."

"I DON'T KNOW ANY OTHER BALL PLAYERS WHO COULD HAVE DONE WHAT HE DID."

—PEE WEE REESE, DODGERS TEAMMATE

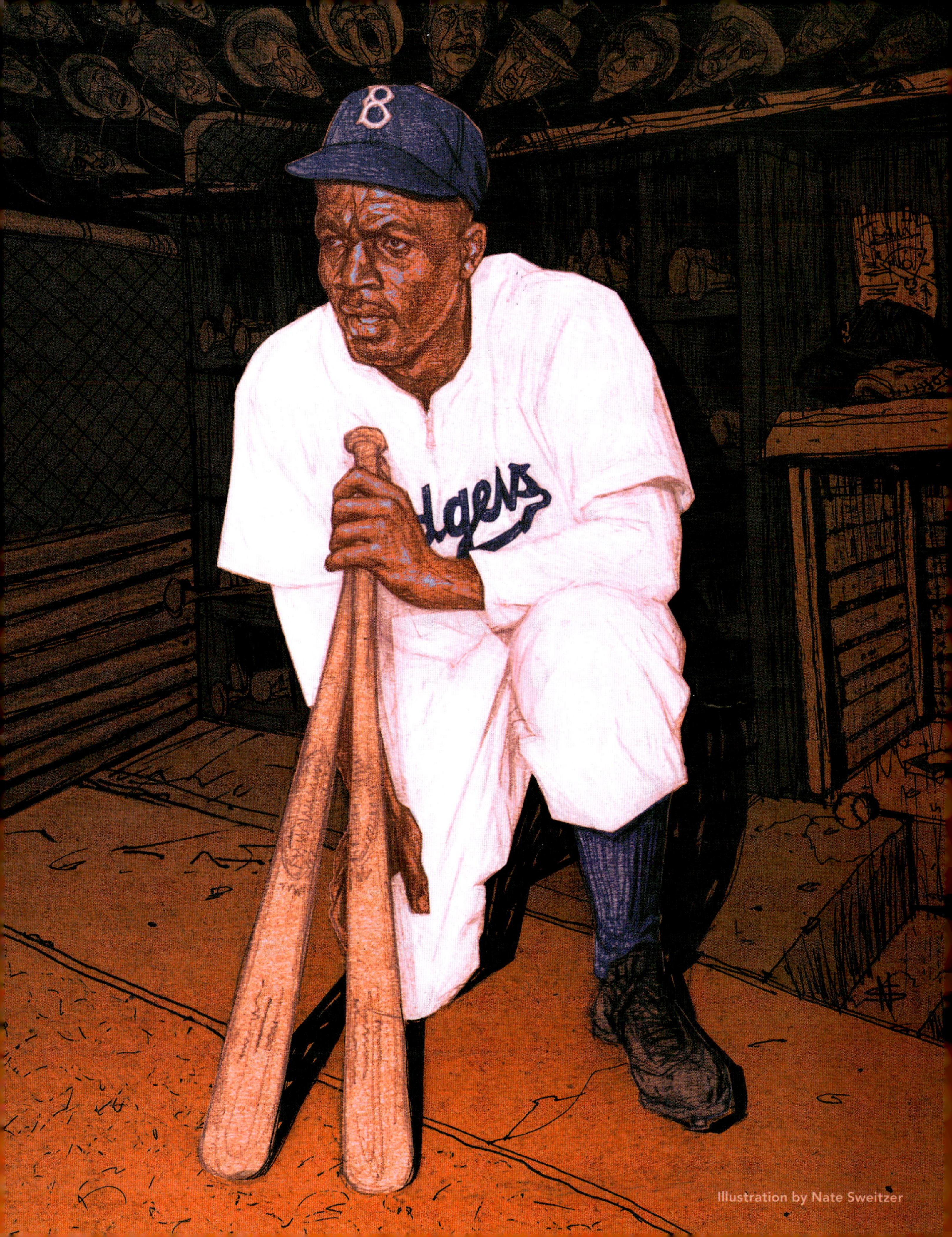

Illustration by Nate Sweitzer

Johann Olav Koss

RIGHT TO PLAY

In the fall of 1993, Norwegian speed skater Johann Olav Koss was preparing for the upcoming Olympic Games in Lillehammer, Norway. He had won two medals in the previous Olympics, but his training was not going well, and he was feeling the pressure of performing in his home country. Johann decided to take a break and do some humanitarian work with Olympic Aid, a newly formed organization assisting war-torn countries in Africa and the Middle East. In September of 1993, he took a week-long trip to Eritrea that would change his life forever.

During that trip, Johann connected with a group of orphans and soon realized that the children needed more than food and shelter. They needed hope and education. "It was a very special trip for me. You focus only on yourself when you are training," Koss said. "Then you visit a place like Eritrea, and you play football with a boy who has one leg, with a ball made out of shirts that are tied together... and I felt the importance of sport." He vowed to the children that after the Olympics, he would return with sports equipment.

Johann went home with a renewed sense of purpose. At the Lillehammer Games, he set three world records and won three gold medals for Norway, becoming a national hero and earning the nickname Koss the Boss. He announced that he would donate his prize money to Olympic Aid, and he urged his fellow Norwegians to contribute as well. By the end of the Games, his countrymen had raised $18 million, and Koss auctioned off his skates for another $90,000. He then asked the families of Norway to donate their extra sports gear and ended up collecting 12 tons of equipment.

Despite the Norwegians' generosity, Johann's work was met with criticism. One newspaper in Norway wrote, "Koss is bringing soccer balls to starving children. What an idiot." But when he returned to Eritrea, the nation's president vindicated Johann, saying, "This is the greatest gift we have ever received. For the first time, we are being treated like human beings—not just something to be kept alive." Koss continued his work for Olympic Aid, ultimately transforming it into Right to Play, a new organization providing aid beyond the Olympic Games. Since 2000, Right to Play has used sport to impact the lives of those in need. Children learn about disease prevention and personal empowerment. School attendance increases. Girls get to participate, even in cultures where they would often be excluded. By giving children around the world the right to play, Koss has nourished them with more than food and water. He has given them knowledge, fun, hope, and he has changed their lives, just as they changed his.

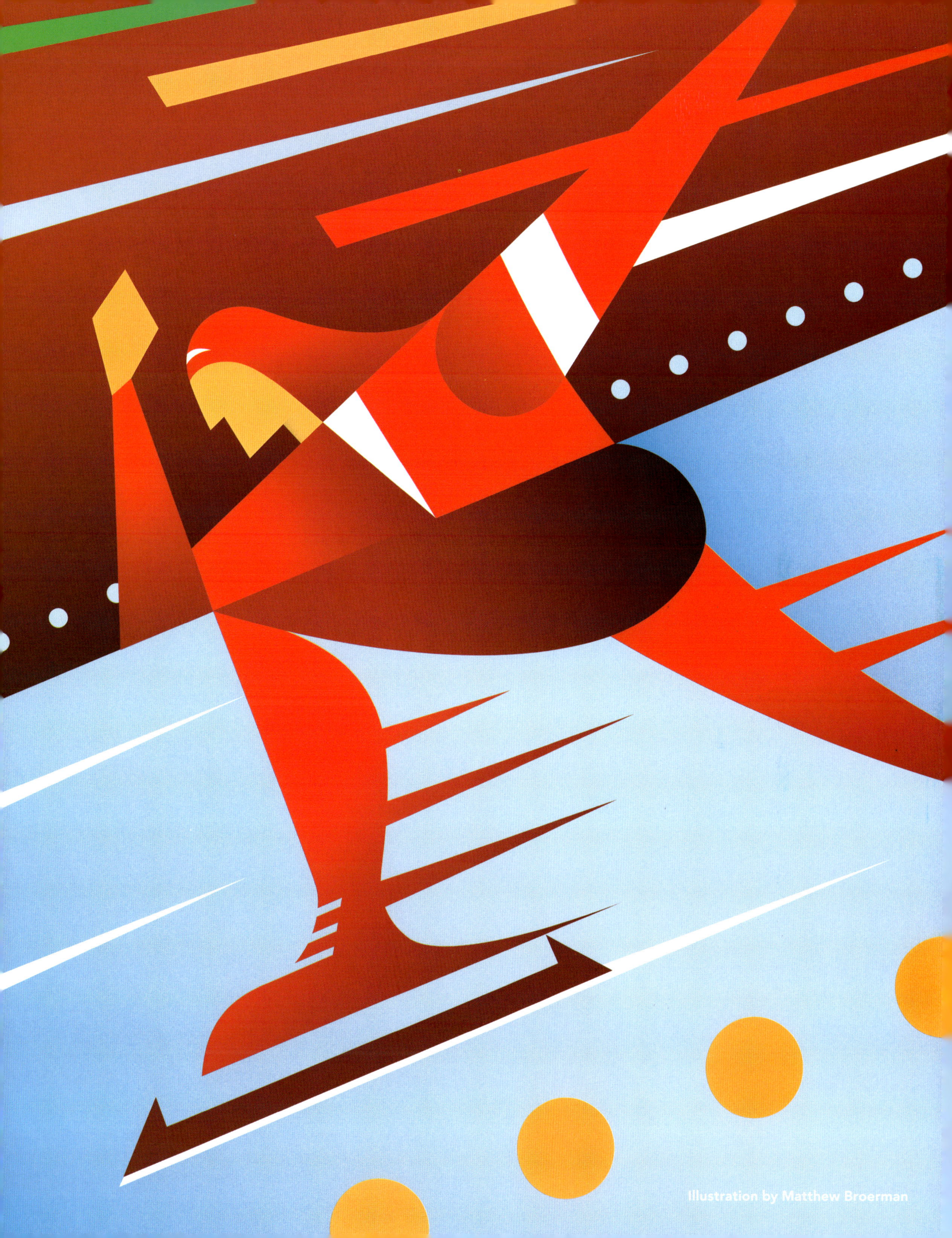

Illustration by Matthew Broerman

John Devitt

TIME-KEEPING TROUBLE

At the 1960 Summer Olympics in Rome, Australian John Devitt and American Lance Larson faced off for the gold medal in the 100-meter freestyle. The two swimmers had recorded the fastest times in qualifying and were placed in lanes next to each other for the final. The race lasted less than a minute, but at the finish, the man with the fastest time wasn't the winner.

All swimming events at the 1960 Games were timed by stopwatch. Three timekeepers stood at the end of each lane, peering over the pool edge to stop their clocks when a swimmer touched the wall. There were also six judges who watched the action and voted for who they thought was the winner. Devitt and Larson were neck and neck the entire race, and it came down to the final meter. Larson realized he couldn't take another stroke before Devitt reached the end, so he stretched out his left arm and touched the wall underwater. Devitt's final stroke touched above the surface. When the timekeepers compared Devitt's time, all three stopwatches read 55.2 seconds. When the timekeepers compared Larson's time, two watches read 55.1, and the other read 55.0. Even though all three of Larson's times were faster than Devitt's, the officials ruled that because of the discrepancy, the winner would be determined by the six judges instead. When the votes were cast, three judges thought Devitt won, and three judges thought Larson won. It was a tie. The head official made the final decision. Both men would be given the time of 55.2, but only Devitt would receive a gold medal and the Olympic record.

As the Australian national anthem played, Larson hung his head. After the race, Devitt said, "At the finish, Larson doesn't know who won it. I don't. The judges were there as far as I'm concerned to decide who won." The US Olympic Team protested the decision for years, but the ruling was never changed.

The Devitt/Larson decision underscored the fallibility of human timekeeping. In 1967, swimming adopted touchpad timers for the Pan American Games, eliminating the need for judges and stopwatches. One year later, the Olympics switched to touchpads, and they've been used ever since. Lance Larson got his gold medal in 1960, as a member of the US 4x100-meter medley relay team, but he'll be remembered for his controversial silver that caused big waves and big changes throughout the sport of swimming.

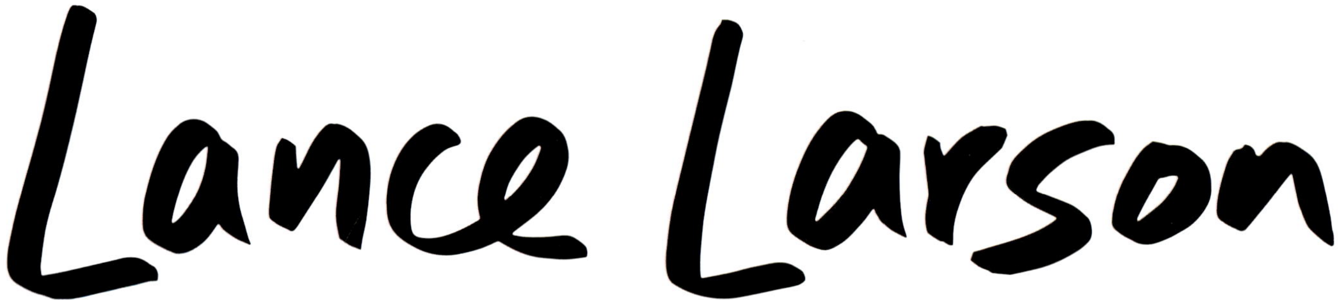

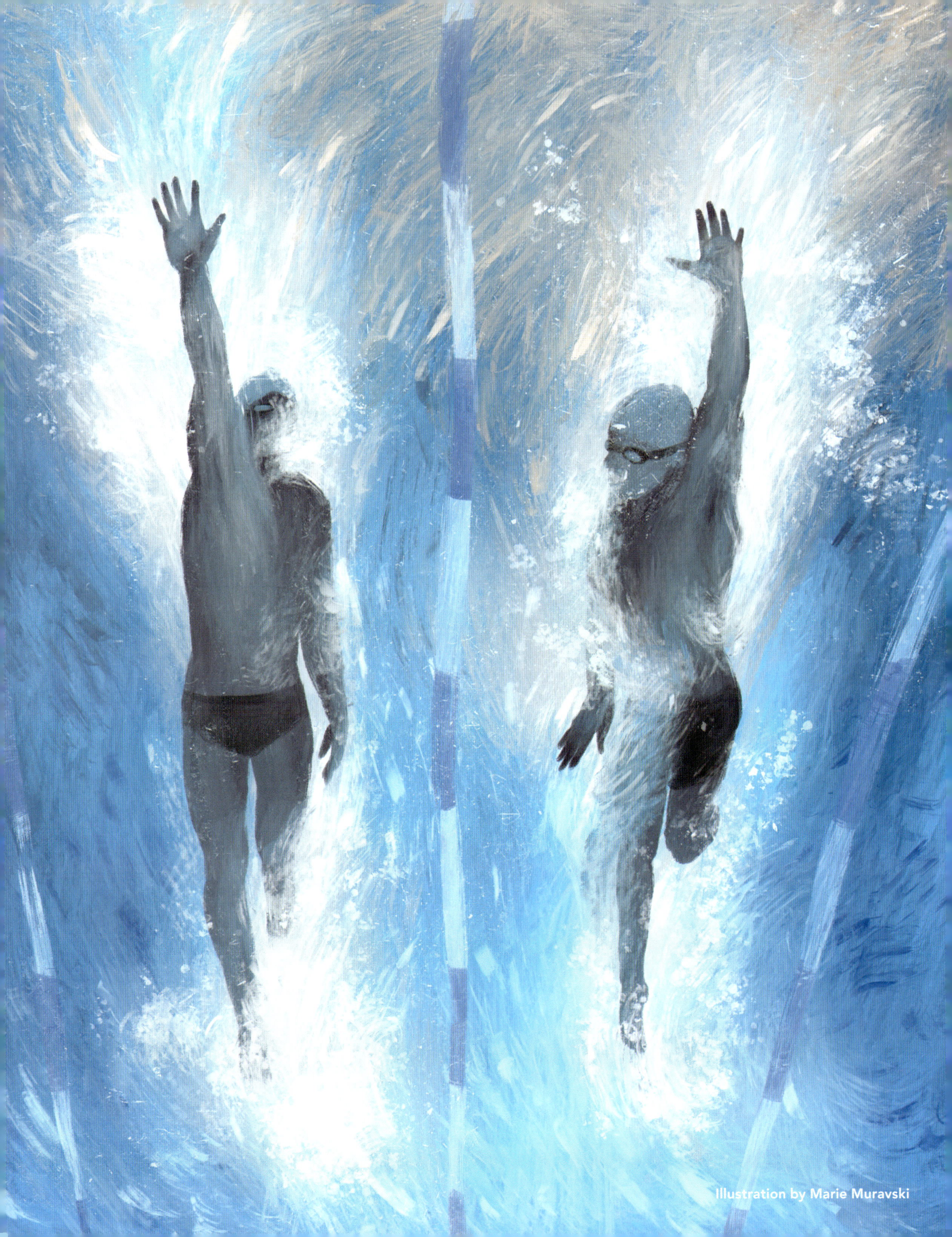

Illustration by Marie Muravski

John Madden

THE GAME MAKER

In the early 1980s, John Madden was the voice of American football to millions of fans. As a Super Bowl-winning coach and NFL analyst, Madden broke down the game week after week with his colorful commentary and catchy phrases. So when video game developer Electronic Arts was looking for a face for their new football game, Madden was one of their top choices. In 1984, Trip Hawkins, founder of EA, and his colleague Joe Ybarra pitched Madden their idea for a football simulator that would be just like the real sport. Due to hardware limitations, Trip suggested limiting the players to seven on each side. "If it's not 11 on 11, it's not real football," Madden spat back. "I'm not putting my name on it if it's not real." With that, John Madden set the course for one of the greatest video game franchises of all time.

Throughout the process, John remained adamant that the game should be as real as possible. He would check in periodically, yelling and screaming about all the details the programmers had wrong. Development dragged on for the next three years—twice as long as the average game. Finally in 1988, *John Madden Football* was released for the Apple II computer. It was marketed as "The First Real Football Simulation," featuring 11 on 11 action and real NFL plays from Madden's time as head coach of the Oakland Raiders. The game had mediocre sales. It ran slowly on the Apple II due to Madden's insistence on 11 players for each side. "We were trying to model NFL football... on a computer with less horsepower than your watch," said Ybarra.

Two years later, EA would try again, releasing *Madden* on the more powerful Sega Genesis system. This time, it was a hit. Bolstered by the success of *Madden*, Electronic Arts created a new division, EA Sports, which went on to develop some of the most successful sports video game franchises of all time, including *NBA Live*, *NHL*, *Tiger Woods PGA Tour*, and *FIFA*. *Madden NFL* became the unrivaled king of football video games, raking in more than $4 billion over 30 years. John's focus on realism continued to propel the series forward year after year. Madden called it "a way for people to learn the game and participate in the game at a pretty sophisticated level." Millions have learned the game from *Madden*. John Madden didn't just change the game—he helped create it. Sportscaster Al Michaels said, "No one has made the sport more interesting, more relevant and more enjoyable to watch and listen to than John."

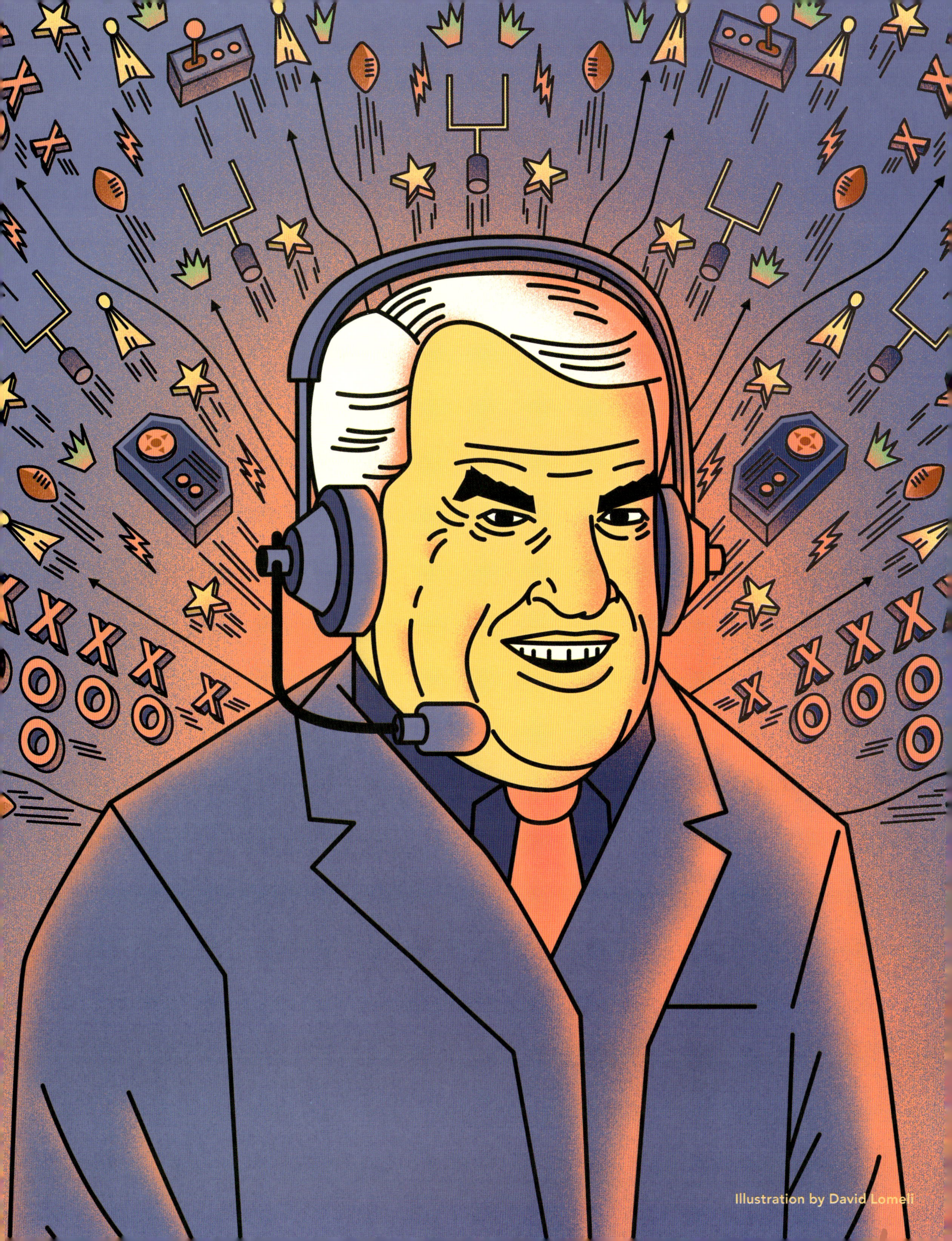

Illustration by David Lomeli

Kareem Abdul-Jabbar

THE NO DUNK RULE

The final game of the 1967 NCAA basketball tournament was a formality for the UCLA Bruins. They entered the game undefeated, 29-0. They had blown away their competition all season long thanks to their star center, 7-foot-2 Lew Alcindor. Before he was known as Kareem Abdul-Jabbar, Lew Alcindor was the most dominant college player the game had ever seen. He was tall, quick, and agile. He dominated both ends of the court, smoothly laying in shots on offense, and swatting balls into the stands on defense. In that final game, Abdul-Jabbar scored 20 points and pulled down 18 rebounds, leading UCLA to a national title. "Kareem could have scored 56 points every night if that had been the objective," said teammate Lynn Shackelford. "What the coaches would do was just tell us to lob the ball into Kareem and him dunk it." Abdul-Jabbar had been dunking since he was 14 years old. It was simply part of how he played the game. Opponents complained he was unstoppable, and that there was no defense against the dunk. The NCAA agreed.

A few days after UCLA's win, the NCAA Rules Committee banned dunking. The committee argued that dunking was dangerous, and players could get injured trying to block dunks. They also stated the dunk was "not a skillful shot" and "upsets the balance between offense and defense." What they meant was Abdul-Jabbar upset the balance, and the ban quickly became known as the "Lew Alcindor Rule." Abdul-Jabbar said, "Of course I was not pleased at having a rule changed just to keep me from playing my best. Part of my passion for basketball was to see how far I could go as an athlete. On the other hand, I was in good company, because two of my role models—Bill Russell and Wilt Chamberlain—had been so dominant, they caused rule changes." UCLA coach John Wooden told Abdul-Jabbar, the rule "is going to make you a better basketball player."

Wooden was right. Abdul-Jabbar pioneered moves like the "skyhook" and led UCLA to two more national titles and an 88-2 combined record. By the time he left college, Kareem Abdul-Jabbar had more national championships than he had losses. He later reminisced, "The dunk ban didn't really end up affecting my overall game much. I'd been perfecting my hook shot since grade school, so I was able to rely more on that. The dunk was reinstated in college ball in 1976, but I was already dunking in the NBA."

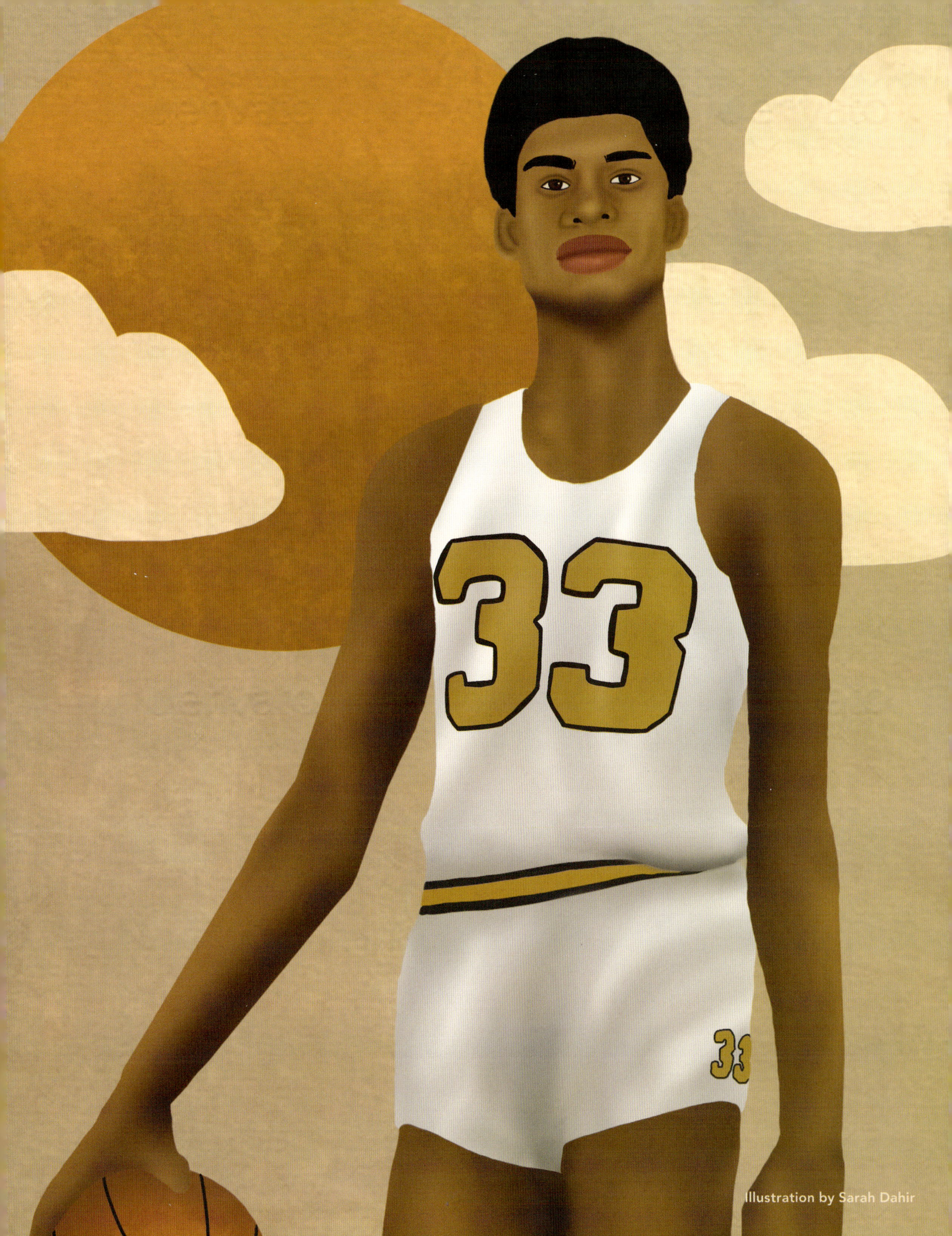

Illustration by Sarah Dahir

"LIFE IS FOR PARTICIPATING, NOT FOR SPECTATING!"

—KATHRINE SWITZER

Kathrine Switzer

Kathrine Switzer wouldn't let anyone stop her from running. When Syracuse University didn't have a women's cross country team, Kathrine ran with the men's team and their coach, Arnie Briggs. As they ran one day in 1966, Arnie reminisced about the Boston Marathon. Kathrine suggested they run the race together. He scoffed, claiming that 26.2 miles was too far for a fragile woman to run. When she challenged Arnie's notion, he declared, "If you ran the distance in practice, I'd be the first to take you to Boston." Kathrine began training, and three weeks before the marathon, she ran 31 miles in practice, proving to Arnie that she was more than ready. Arnie agreed, and they planned their trip to Boston.

On April 19, 1967, Kathrine stood among more than 700 men gathered at the start of the race. As she pinned on her #261 bib, Switzer became the first woman to officially compete in the Boston Marathon. Alongside her for this historic moment were Arnie and her boyfriend, Tom Miller. As the race started, there was a buzz among the male competitors about the woman in their midst. Around mile four, conservative race official Jock Semple got wind of the controversial news. He stormed onto the course, grabbing at Kathrine's bib, shouting, "Get the hell out of my race and give me those numbers!" Shocked and terrified, she kept running as Tom knocked Jock to the ground. A press truck full of journalists and photographers sped alongside them. Reporters began shouting questions, "What are you trying to prove?" and "When are you going to quit?" Infuriated, Switzer understood the enormity of what she was doing and the importance of finishing the marathon. She told Arnie, "I have to finish this race... I have to—even on my hands and knees."

Kathrine ran on, with broken blisters and bloodied socks, crossing the finish line in 4 hours, 20 minutes. The press had followed her all day, and the story of her tenacity and athleticism was in the newspapers the next morning. Kathrine's race in 1967 still resonates with runners today. Switzer said, "When I go to the Boston Marathon now, I have wet shoulders—women fall into my arms crying. They're weeping for joy because running has changed their lives. They feel they can do anything."

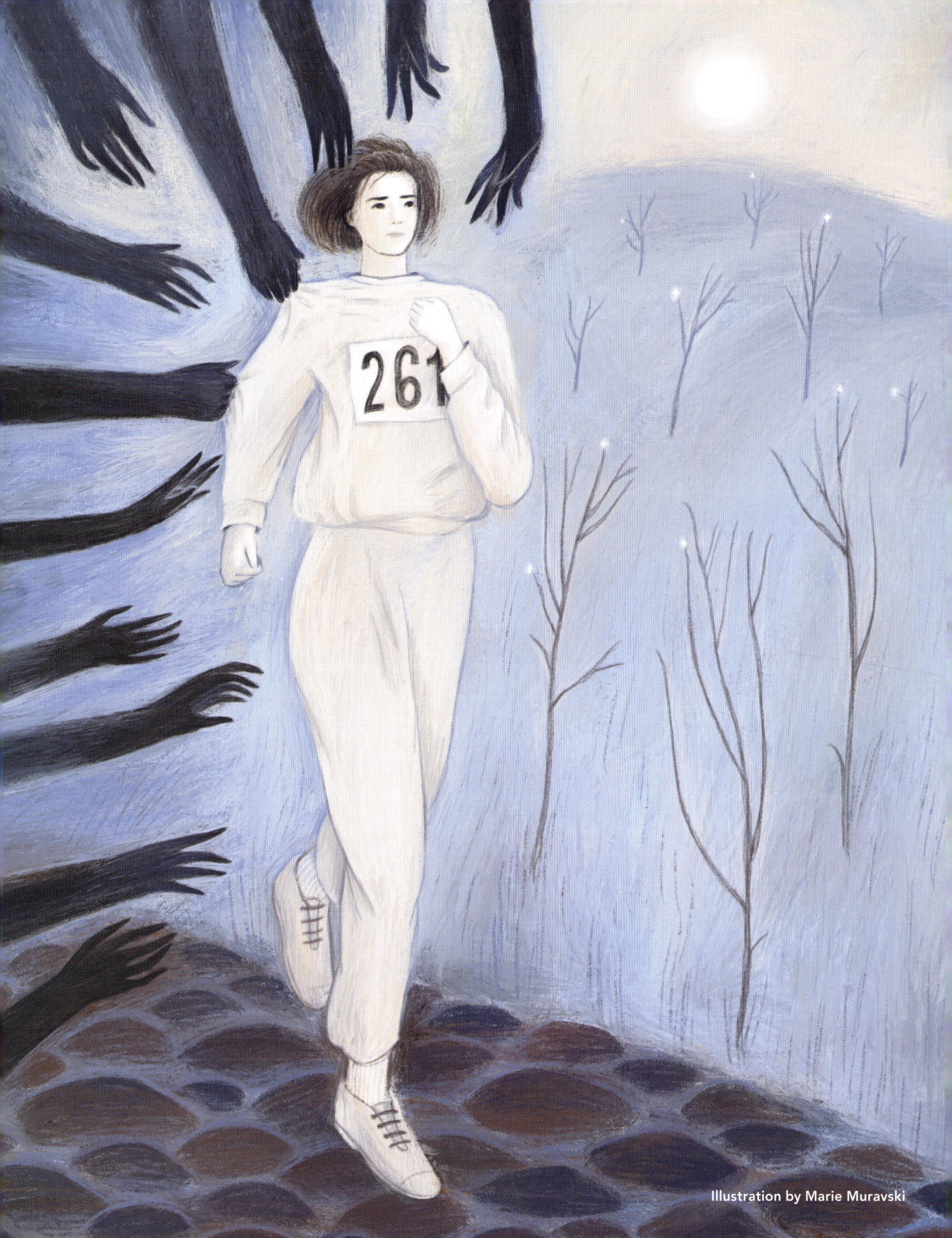

Illustration by Marie Muravski

Kenny Sailors

Thirteen-year-old Kenny Sailors was tired of losing to his older brother Bud in basketball. Bud relished beating his younger—and smaller—brother in one-on-one. Kenny recalled, "I never could get a shot off, and he really enjoyed that because he was 6-foot-5, and I was just about, I don't know, 5-foot-7 probably. He used to tell me, 'You better find another game. This isn't your game. It's for big men, tall men.'" But one spring day in 1934, little Kenny had an idea. He dribbled up to his brother, jumped into the air, and released a shot high above his head. His brother, standing flat-footed, was dumbfounded, saying, "Kenny, you may have something there. You better develop that shot."

Kenny did develop it, creating basketball's first jump shot. Sailors was a standout player at the University of Wyoming, leading his team to an NCAA championship in 1943. "People out East, had heard stories about this team from the West, and their superstar who played this kind of crazy game," said sports author Shawn Fury. Basketball players of that era were taught to stay on the ground and not get caught in the air. "They would raise a hand to try to block the shot, but a lot of times they wouldn't jump," Fury said. The success of the jump shot led Sailors to the NBA. His first coach, Dutch Dehnert, didn't care for Kenny's shot. In his heavy New York accent, Dutch asked Kenny, "Where'd youse get that leapin' one-hander?" He continued, "You just never make it in this league with that kind of a shot." Fortunately for Kenny, it was Dutch who didn't make it. He was fired midway through the 1946-47 season, and new coach Roy Clifford embraced Kenny's technique. The jump shot took off across the league, and with it, scoring exploded. Fury said, "You know, you used to have games in the 40s or the 50s. Now you had games in the 80s and 90s. And fans just enjoyed that more." Many assume the jump shot was always part of the game, but it was a boy from Wyoming who paved the way for great shooters like Jerry West, Ray Allen, and Steph Curry. Kenny Sailors revolutionized the sport, especially for the little guy. Curry said, "I can't play above the rim, so the jump shot is my only weapon." In 2012, nearly 80 years after his first jump shot, Kenny Sailors was inducted into the National Collegiate Basketball Hall of Fame.

"YOU BETTER FIND ANOTHER GAME. THIS ISN'T YOUR GAME. IT'S FOR BIG MEN, TALL MEN."

—BUD SAILORS, KENNY'S BROTHER

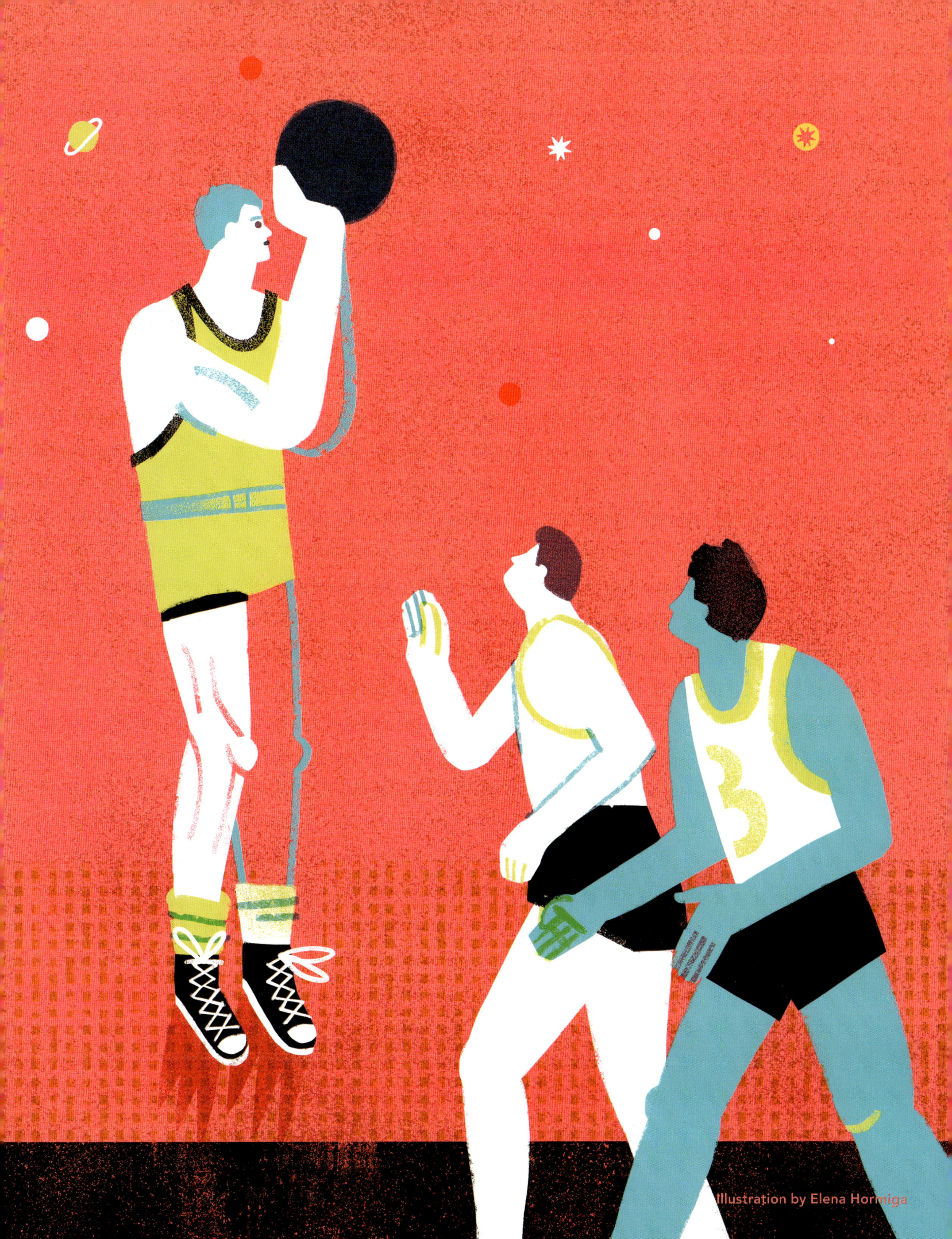

Illustration by Elena Hormiga

"IF YOU CAN INCLUDE MORE PEOPLE, ISN'T THAT THE WHOLE ATTITUDE OF THE SPORT?"

—KULSOOM ABDULLAH

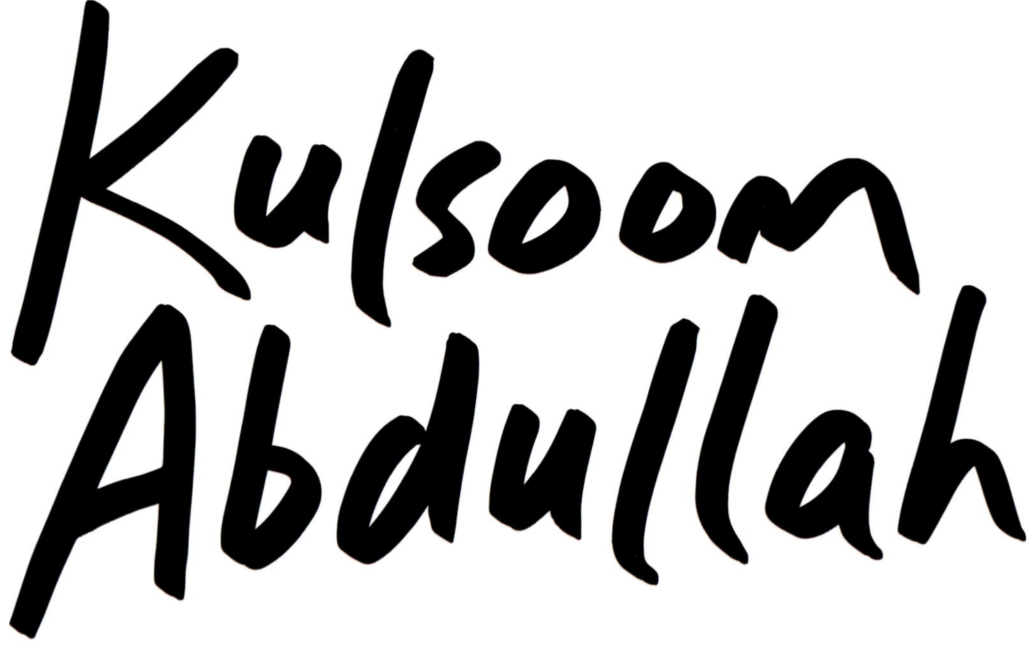

Kulsoom Abdullah was pursuing her master's degree in computer engineering when she first took up weightlifting. Soon, lifting became her passion. "I found it addictive... not just physically but also psychologically," said Abdullah.

Kulsoom was a devout Muslim. Her parents had immigrated to the United States from Pakistan before she was born. When she was a teenager, Abdullah started wearing a hijab head covering and modest dress in keeping with her faith. "I am a Muslim who tries to implement as many of Islam's teachings as possible in my daily life," she said. "Modesty is one of those teachings, and I choose to honor it when I cover in public." In 2010, she qualified for the USA Weightlifting National Championships and was excited to compete in her first national tournament. But she was told she would not be allowed to participate unless she wore a singlet—a form-fitting uniform exposing her arms and legs. The International Weightlifting Federation argued that judges needed to see the knees and elbows of competitors to determine if they had completed their lifts. Abdullah was forced to choose between her religion and her passion. Instead, she hired a lawyer and won the support of the Council for American-Islamic Relations and the US Olympic Committee. She even submitted designs for alternative uniforms that would adhere to her religious code while still allowing officials to accurately judge her lifts. Her story garnered national attention, shining a light on issues of persecution, religious tolerance, and individual freedom. In June 2011, the IWF changed its rules, allowing Abdullah to compete in a hijab and a full-body unitard underneath the traditional singlet. John Duff, CEO of USA Weightlifting, called Abdullah's participation a key milestone and a step forward for inclusion within weightlifting. That same year, Kulsoom became the first woman to compete for Pakistan in the World Weightlifting Championships.

Abdullah's victory sent a shockwave through the world of sports. The 2012 and 2016 Olympic Games saw a record number of athletes proudly wearing religious head coverings. Athletes including runner Sarah Attar, volleyball player Doaa Elghobashy, figure skater Zahra Lari, and fencer Ibtihaj Muhammad have become symbols of diversity, inclusion, and tolerance. Abdullah said, "I hope other sporting organizations will follow this example to allow greater inclusion and participation in their respective sport."

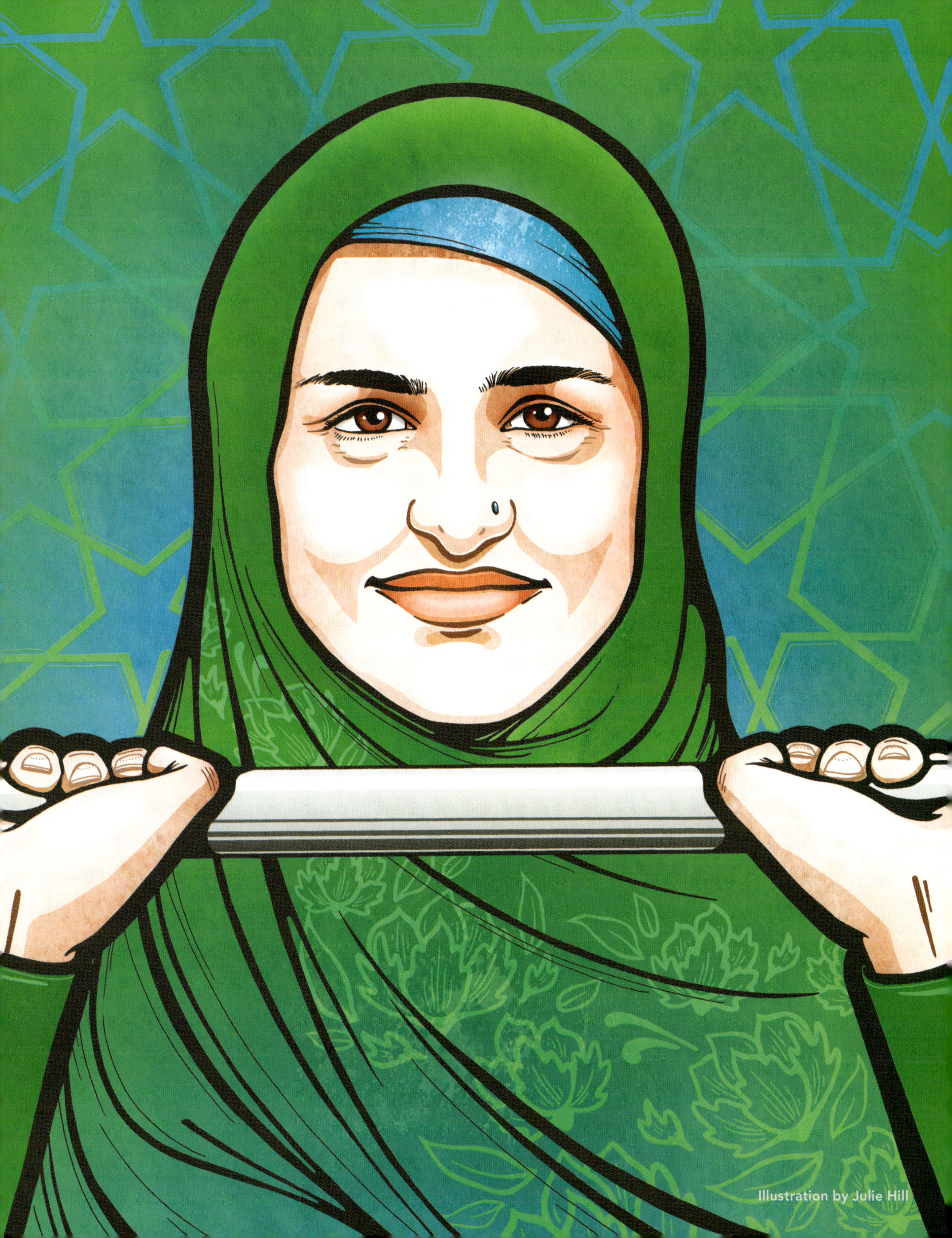
Illustration by Julie Hill

Ludwig Guttmann

Jewish doctor Ludwig Guttmann was a top neurosurgeon in Germany during the 1930s. When the Nazis seized control of the country, they banned Jews from practicing medicine. Fearing for his life, Guttmann fled to London. War broke out across Europe. Millions died, and millions more were severely injured. Soldiers returned home battered and broken. In 1943, the British government asked Guttmann to establish a new hospital for veterans left paralyzed by the fighting.

The Stoke Mandeville Hospital Spinal Injuries Center began receiving its first patients in 1944. At the time, paralyzed patients were confined to their beds, heavily sedated, and shut away from society. Infections and bedsores were rampant, and most individuals withered away within two years. But Guttmann pioneered a new therapeutic approach. He required each of his patients to participate in crafts and activities. He introduced sports and set up competitions. On July 29, 1948, the same day as the opening of the London Summer Olympics, Guttmann invited patients from neighboring hospitals to compete in an archery contest at Stoke Mandeville. The 16 competitors that day became the first Paralympians. Ludwig described the importance of the games, "Not everyone can be a sporting star, but if a newly disabled person coming to terms with their injury can see people taking part in sport here it can inspire them and shows them what they can do." Guttmann held his competitions every year. In 1952, the first international group joined Ludwig's games when patients from the Netherlands competed. In 1960, the games moved to Rome and marked the first time the Olympics and Paralympics were held in the same city. That year, 400 disabled athletes from 23 countries competed. The Paralympics have been held every Olympic year since. Guttmann saw sports as important to his patients' physical and mental health, and the Paralympic Games as a tool for acceptance. "In those days being in a wheelchair was a constant struggle, you just had to accept you couldn't do a lot of things or go to a lot of places," said Sally Haynes, one of Guttmann's patients and a competitor in the 1964 Tokyo Paralympics. "Guttmann was always telling us we were pioneers, we were leading the way."

In 2012, the Olympics were once again held in London, and the Paralympics followed shortly after. 4,200 athletes from 164 countries competed in Dr. Guttmann's vision. His work revolutionized the care of the paralyzed and championed their inclusion into society. Haynes said, "I think the world has accepted us now. I didn't ever think we would get this far."

"GUTTMANN WAS ALWAYS TELLING US WE WERE PIONEERS."

—SALLY HAYNES, PARALYMPIAN

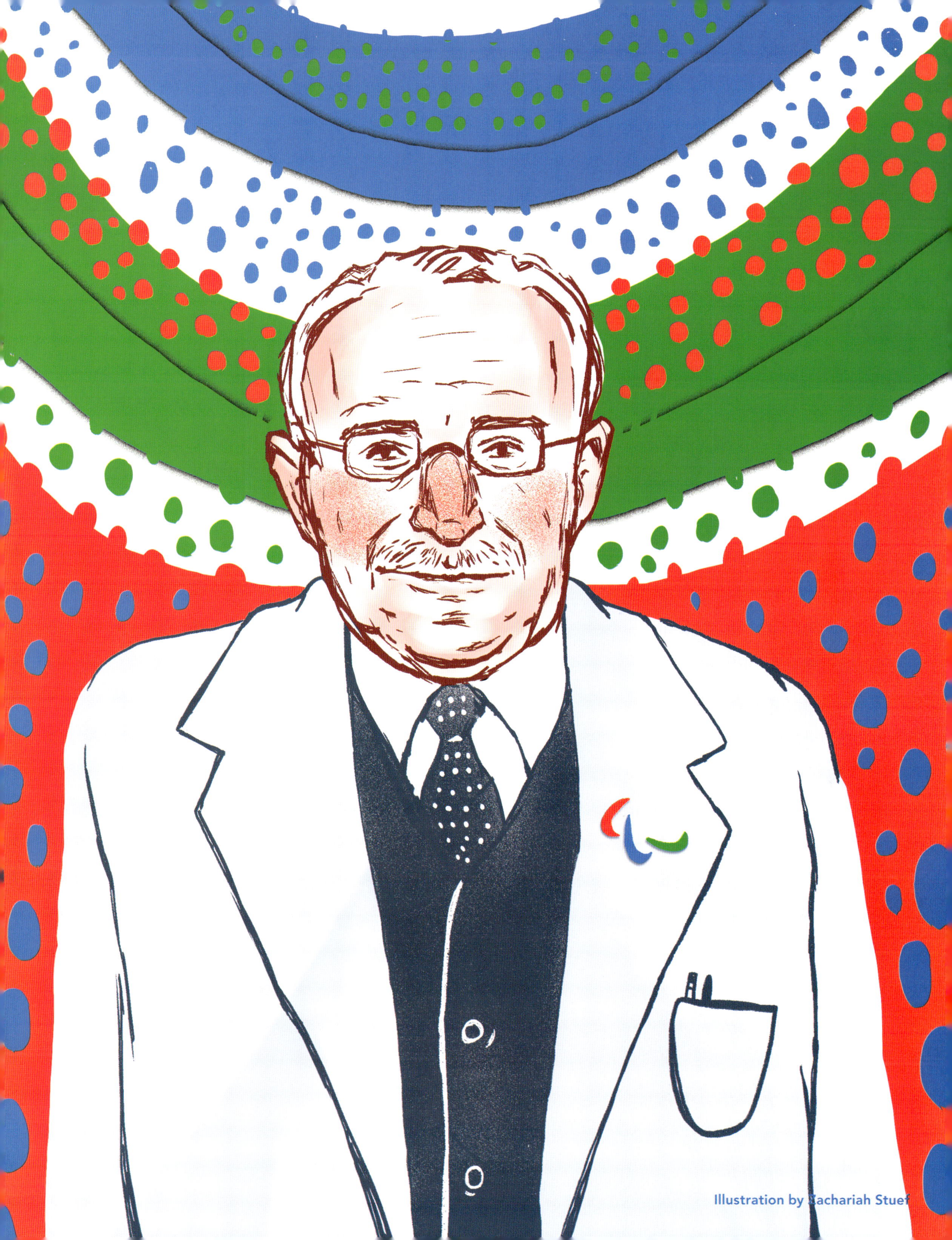

Illustration by Sachariah Stuef

Magic Johnson

Magic Johnson solemnly stood behind the podium during a surprise press conference on November 7, 1991. Johnson started to speak but hesitated in a way he never had on the basketball court. He looked out across the sea of reporters, collected his thoughts, and made an announcement that shocked the world. "Because of the HIV virus I have attained, I will have to retire from the Lakers today." Next to Magic was NBA commissioner David Stern, who had learned about the diagnosis from a phone call earlier. Stern remembered, "I froze. I didn't really have an immediate reaction. I had to think about how to respond. It was horrified grief about Magic's prospects for living. I thought Magic was going to die. Everyone did. That was the nature of HIV/AIDS in this country at the time." But with his trademark smile, Johnson offered hope, saying, "I plan to go on, living for a long time, buggin' you guys like I always have."

At that press conference, Magic Johnson became the public face of HIV/AIDS in America. He could have retired without a word of explanation. He'd played 12 seasons and had already won five NBA championships and three MVPs. Instead, Magic chose to announce his diagnosis and lead a group of people stigmatized and in need of a champion. That same year, he established the Magic Johnson Foundation, a non-profit dedicated to HIV/AIDS awareness and research. Johnson began treatment and briefly, but controversially, returned to basketball, playing in the 1992 Olympics and the 1995-96 NBA season. He continued to advocate for HIV/AIDS awareness, working with the US Congress as part of the National Commission on AIDS under President George H.W. Bush and speaking at the UN for World AIDS Day in 1999. Although still a devastating illness, HIV/AIDS is no longer the killer it once was. Johnson is credited with taking the disease out of the shadows and increasing funding, research, and testing rates.

After decades of progress, now like Magic, millions are living with, rather than dying from, this disease. On November 7, 2016, the 25th anniversary of his famed press conference, Johnson wrote on his website, "Today is a celebration of life, a celebration of what some people thought was a death sentence 25 years ago. It's a celebration of everything I've been through until now."

> *"I THOUGHT MAGIC WAS GOING TO DIE. EVERYONE DID. THAT WAS THE NATURE OF HIV/AIDS IN THIS COUNTRY AT THE TIME."*
>
> —DAVID STERN, NBA COMMISSIONER

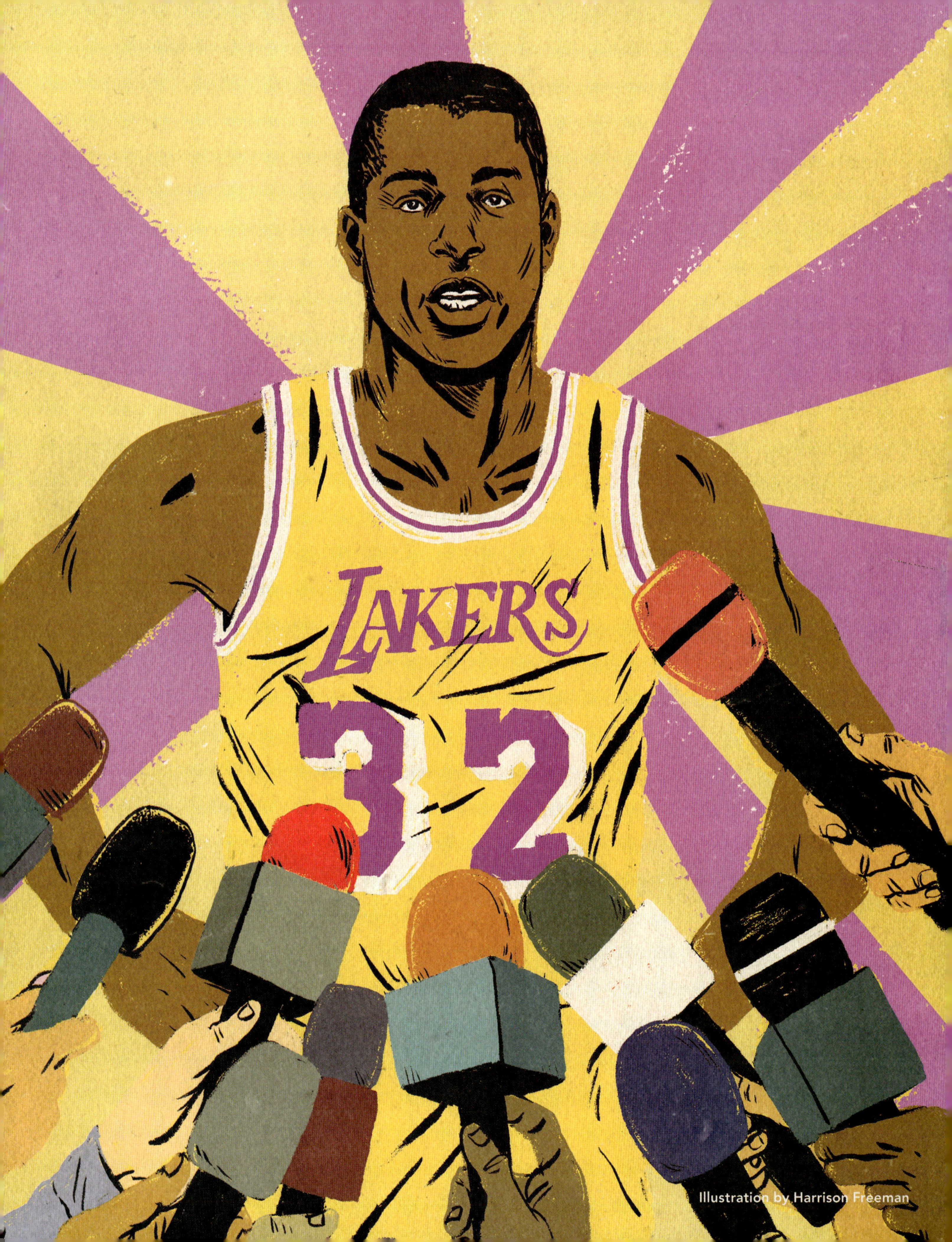

Illustration by Harrison Freeman

Martin Brodeur

THE TRAPEZOID

In the third period of a 1997 playoff game against the Montreal Canadiens, New Jersey Devils goalkeeper Martin Brodeur fielded the puck from behind the net. He skated out and launched a shot toward the opposing goal. The puck flew through the air, landed past center ice, and slid into the Canadiens net. Gooooaaaal! The sirens blared, and the Devils went on to win 5-2.

Brodeur wasn't the only goalie to score in the NHL, but he did it the most. For a goalkeeper, Martin was particularly adept at puck handling, a skill inspired by seeing Ron Hextall skate out from the net and field the puck. Brodeur recalled, "I watched a game and saw him play and I was amazed and I thought, 'You know what, that's what I want to do, I want to put that in my game.' And so I started working at it." Former Devils teammate Mike McKenna said, "He could do more than stop the puck and occasionally clear the zone. His intelligence and awareness allowed him to make plays. Passes, chips, clears, bumps, delays; Marty could do it all." Brodeur played the position beautifully, skating out, handling the puck, and functioning like a third defensemen for the Devils. New Jersey won three Stanley Cups with Brodeur in the net. Then in 2004, a labor dispute between the NHL and its players canceled the 2004-2005 season. When hockey resumed the following year, the NHL had changed some rules, including one targeted at Brodeur. Instead of allowing goalies to freely handle the puck anywhere behind the goal line, keepers would be limited to a small "trapezoid" shape directly behind the net. Since Martin was one of the few goalies who handled the puck, the rule quickly became known as the "Brodeur Rule."

Brodeur was furious. "You can't be happy, taking away something I've worked on all my life to do and help my teammates and help my defense," he exclaimed. "It's just part of me, playing the puck." The NHL claimed the new rule would increase scoring and keep hockey from becoming a "tennis match." Despite losing one of his primary weapons, Martin Brodeur continued his Hall of Fame career. He holds the records for most saves, most shutouts, and most wins as a goalie. He won four Vezina trophies and two Olympic gold medals. The trapezoid is one of hockey's most maligned rule changes. After more than a decade in use, there has been little evidence that it increases scoring or does anything other than frustrate skilled goalkeepers. In 2015, after his retirement, Brodeur said, "The trapezoid has to go."

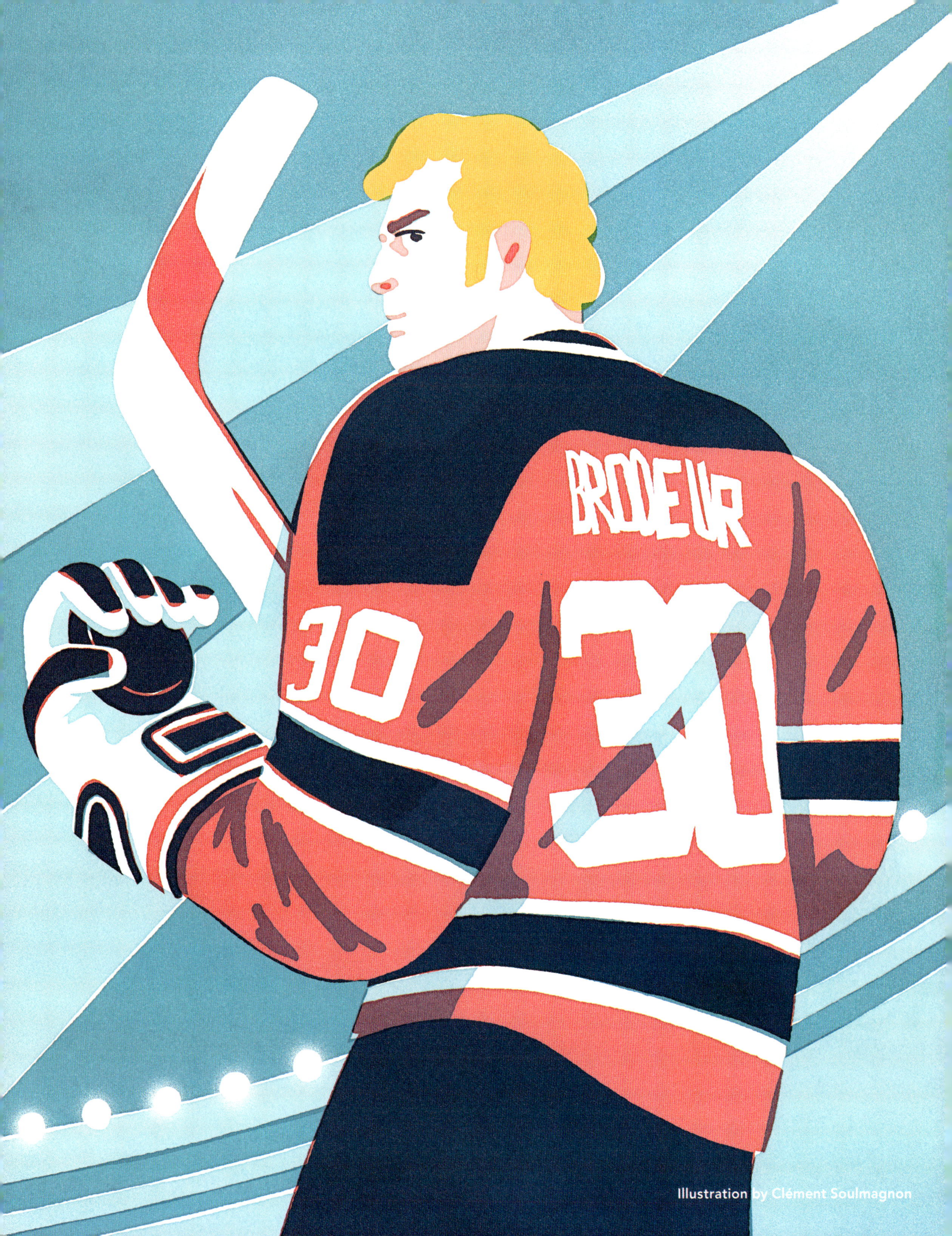

Illustration by Clément Soulmagnon

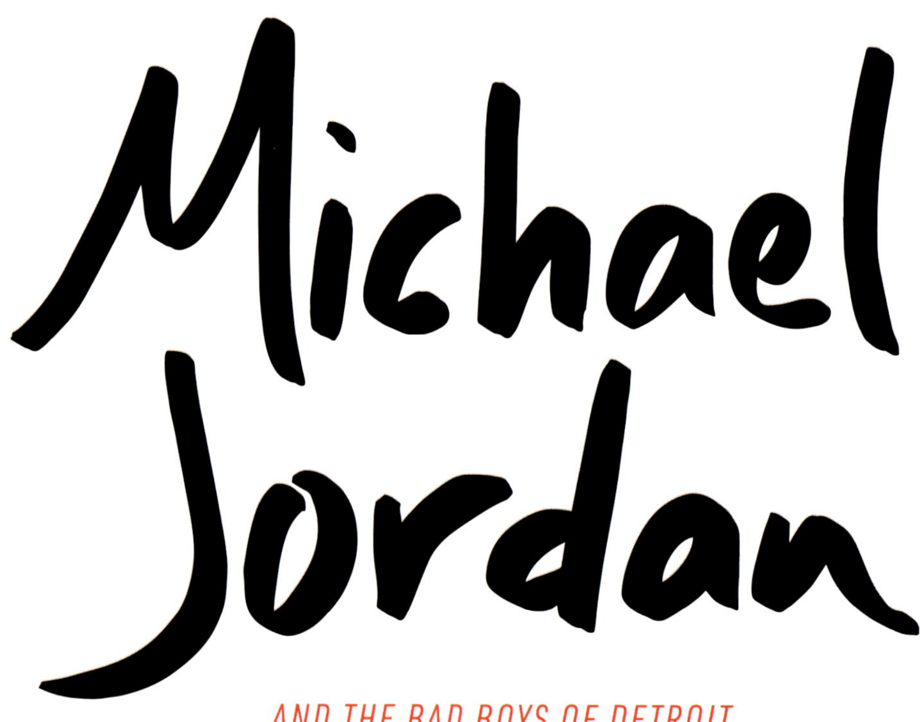

AND THE BAD BOYS OF DETROIT

After only four years in the NBA, Michael Jordan had accumulated an impressive list of personal accolades: Rookie of the Year, Scoring Champion, Defensive Player of the Year, and MVP. He was good, very good, but he wasn't yet great. To be considered great, Jordan would need the one thing that eluded him—a championship. To get it, he'd have to change his attitude, change his game, and go through the toughest team in NBA history, the "Bad Boys" of Detroit.

The 1988 Detroit Pistons earned their bad boy nickname. They terrorized opponents with insults and elbows. Games often erupted into full-blown fights, and they never backed down, especially to Jordan and the Chicago Bulls. The Pistons hated losing to Michael, so to defeat the Bulls, they created a strategy known as the "Jordan Rules." The Jordan Rules were designed to keep Michael in check, beating him mentally and physically. Piston's forward Dennis Rodman remembered, "When he goes to the basket, he ain't gonna dunk. We're gonna hit you and you're gonna be on the ground. We were trying to physically hurt Michael." The Pistons knocked the Bulls out of the playoffs in 1988, 1989, and 1990. After the Bulls lost in the 1990 Eastern Conference Finals, Jordan cried on the bus. But the emotion stoked his competitive fire. "I was getting brutally beaten up," Jordan recalled. "I wanted to start fighting back." He hit the gym, putting on 15 pounds of muscle. He expanded his game beyond flamboyant drives and acrobatic finishes. He honed a mid-range jumper and a fade-away that would become iconic Jordan. And he embraced the concept of team, relying on his teammates to make big shots in big moments.

In 1991, the Pistons and the Bulls met again in the Eastern Conference Finals. This time, the bad boys were no match for the new Jordan and the new Bulls. The Jordan Rules were inconsequential, and Chicago swept Detroit in four games. Jordan and the Bulls went on to win their first NBA championship. After winning the title, Michael cried tears of victory. "No one can ever take this away from me," he said. "This has been a seven-year struggle for me." Breaking through Detroit, Jordan's greatness continued to rise. Three straight championships, then three more. Five league MVPs and 10 scoring titles. Jordan was forged in the fires of Detroit, sharpened mentally and physically, and reborn as a player and a leader. Magic Johnson said of Michael, "The reason he became the GOAT is because he had to go through the Pistons."

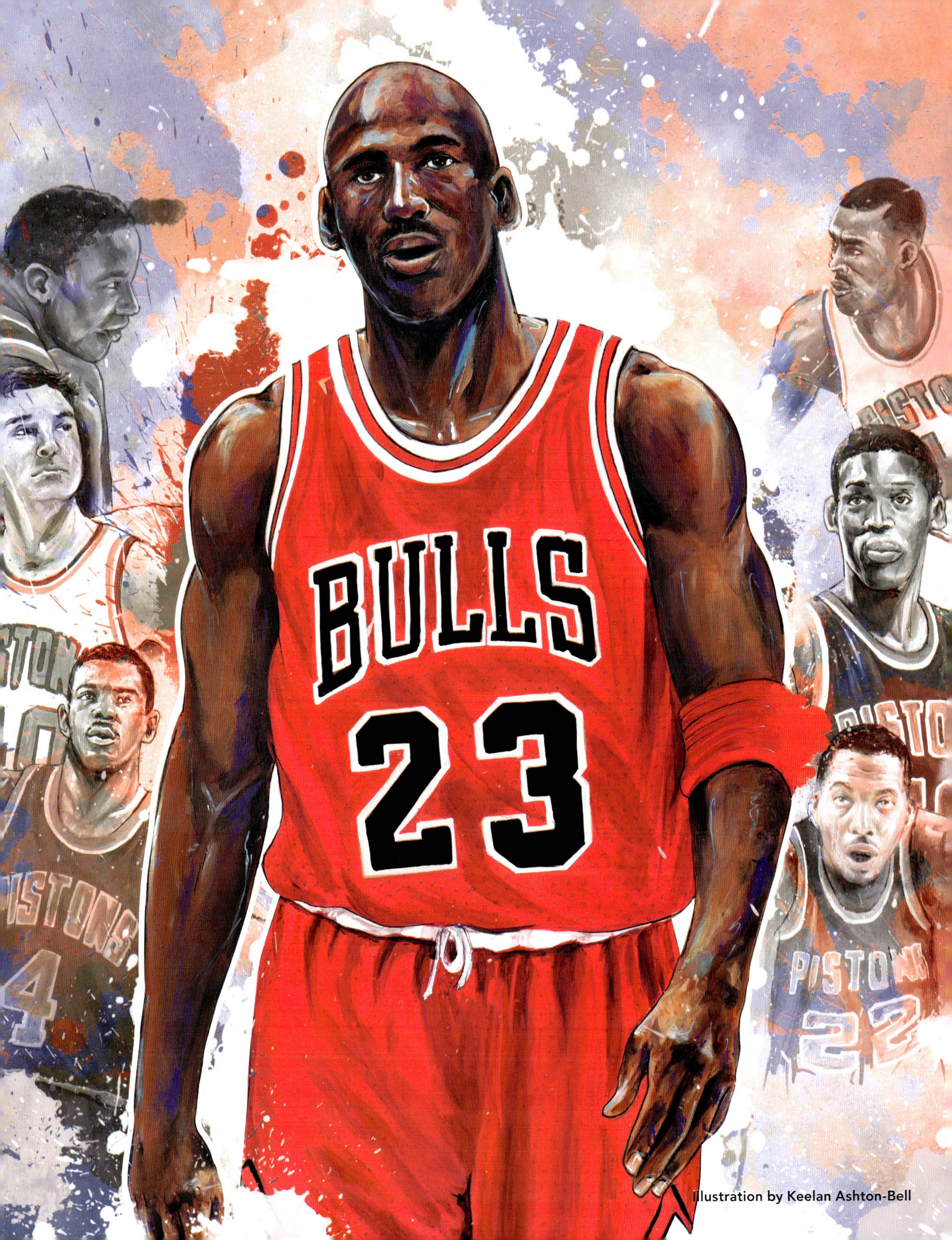

Illustration by Keelan Ashton-Bell

Mirosław Graf

THE FLYING V

In the two centuries since it began, ski jumping has morphed from winter pastime into daredevil sport. Jumpers launch themselves 300 feet through the air, reaching speeds of 60 mph before attempting to land on two narrow skis. "It's basically as close as you can get to flying," said US jumper Michael Glasder. Others have described it as "falling with style."

Style is an important factor. Competitive jumps are judged not only by distance but also by technique. Three popular styles emerged in the early-to-mid-20th century: the Kongsberger, Windisch, and Däscher techniques. Kongsberger jumpers flew off the ramp in a Superman pose with both arms outstretched. Windisch and Däscher jumpers pulled their arms to their sides as they tried to create a more aerodynamic shape. In all three styles, the jumpers' skis were parallel and underneath their bodies. The judges considered these techniques as stylish ways to jump. But around 1969, a young Polish boy named Mirosław Graf accidentally discovered a new technique. Graf was recovering from a sprained ankle, and he couldn't keep the traditional forms when he jumped. As the youngster flew through the air, his weak ankle caused his skis to flare out, forming a V-shape. His coaches recommended adding braces to his ski bindings to help correct his form, but with the V-shape, Mirosław found he was actually flying farther. He continued to hone his style and began using it in competitions. Unfortunately, the judges thought Graf's technique was ugly, and they routinely deducted style points, costing him victories. In a competition in Karpacz, Poland, Graf performed the longest jump but placed only fourth. He set distance records throughout Poland and Germany. Despite the longer jumps, Mirosław never gained much success because judges continued to penalize his technique. Graf unceremoniously retired in 1982, but the V-style lived on with Swedish jumper Jan Boklöv.

For Boklöv, the distance advantage of the V could not be ignored. He insisted on using the technique in competition, knowing he would lose points. Even with the penalty, Jan dominated ski jumping in the late '80s, winning five World Cup events and becoming the Swedish national champion from 1985-1990. A few years later, the V-style became recognized as a valid form and was no longer penalized. Since then, the V-style, or Graf-Boklöv style, has become the most widely used technique in ski jumping, shattering records, and sending daredevils flying faster and farther than ever before.

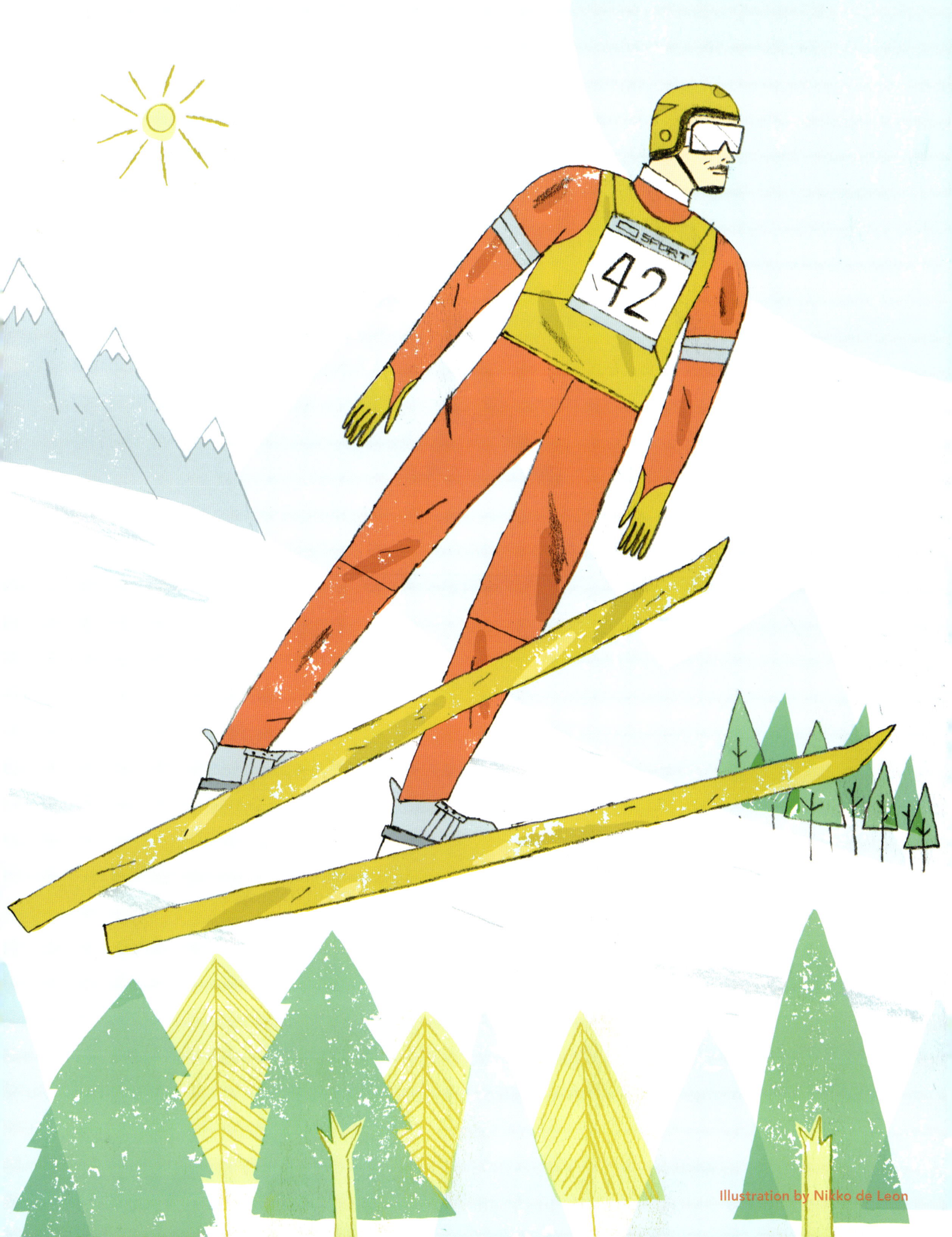

Illustration by Nikko de Leon

Muhammad Ali

THE PEOPLE'S CHAMP

Part sportsman. Part showman. Part activist. Sociologist Harry Edwards called Muhammad Ali "the father of the modern athlete." In a world of imitators, Ali was the originator.

Muhammad Ali was born Cassius Clay and grew up as a have-not in segregated Louisville, Kentucky. He was surrounded by White-only parks, White-only stores, and White-only restaurants. "I wanted to be a big celebrity," he said. "So that I could rebel and be different from all the rest of them and show everyone behind me that you don't have to be Uncle Tom, you don't have to kiss-you-know-what to make it.... I wanted to be free. I wanted to say what I wanna say... go where I wanna go. Do what I wanna do." He found his opportunity in boxing—training hard, fighting, and winning a gold medal at the 1960 Olympics. Thinking he finally made it, Ali wore his medal to a restaurant in downtown Louisville. A waitress approached and said, "We don't serve Negroes here." Enraged, he quipped back, "I don't eat 'em, either, just give me a cup of coffee and a hot dog!" He was turned away, and then he threw his gold medal into the Ohio River.

Ali's star continued to rise. He sought money and fame, and he got his chance at both in a 1964 title fight against heavyweight champion Sonny Liston. The whole world predicted Ali's defeat. After all, many said he "fought all wrong." He held his hands to his sides, leaned back to avoid punches, and lacked knockout power. What Ali did have was speed—and lots of it. When the opening bell rang, Ali floated around Liston, snapping jabs at the champ's face. Sonny was outplayed. After seven rounds, he called it quits, and Ali took the heavyweight crown. That night, Ali announced he "shook up the world." The next day, he delivered an aftershock. He proclaimed his allegiance to the radical Nation of Islam and sloughed off his "slave name" of Cassius Clay in favor of Muhammad Ali. If the masses were looking for a stoic Black champion, they wouldn't find it in Ali. He assaulted long-held views of race and religion. He refused to fight in the Vietnam War, which he saw as bigoted and unjust. He was stripped of his title, banned from boxing for more than three years, and threatened with imprisonment. He was labeled a draft-dodger, a loudmouth, a hero, and a villain. Ali stood against oppression, fighting for what he believed was right. Former heavyweight champ and Ali opponent George Foreman said, "He was such a great man, boxing should be the last thing you want to remember about him."

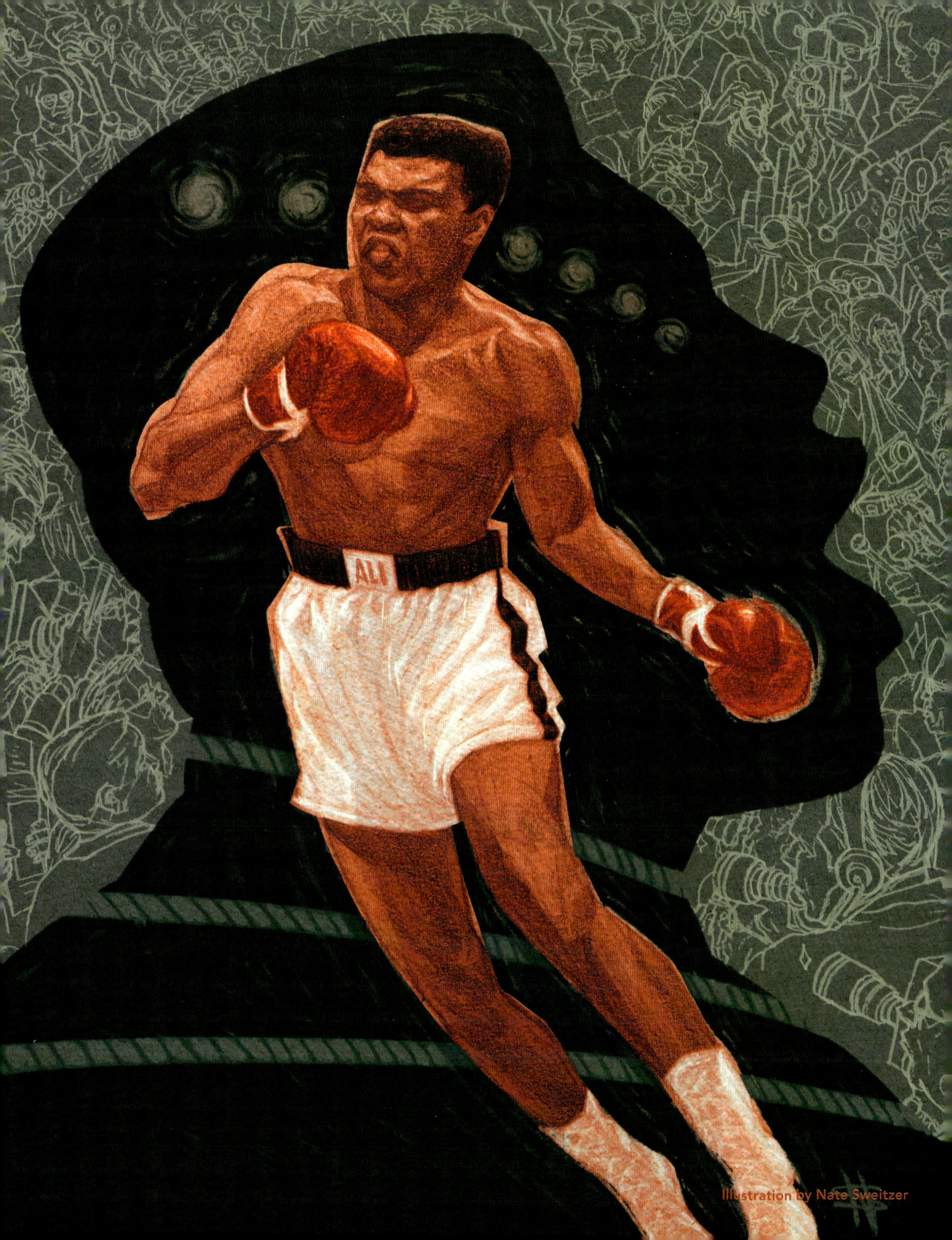

Illustration by Nate Sweitzer

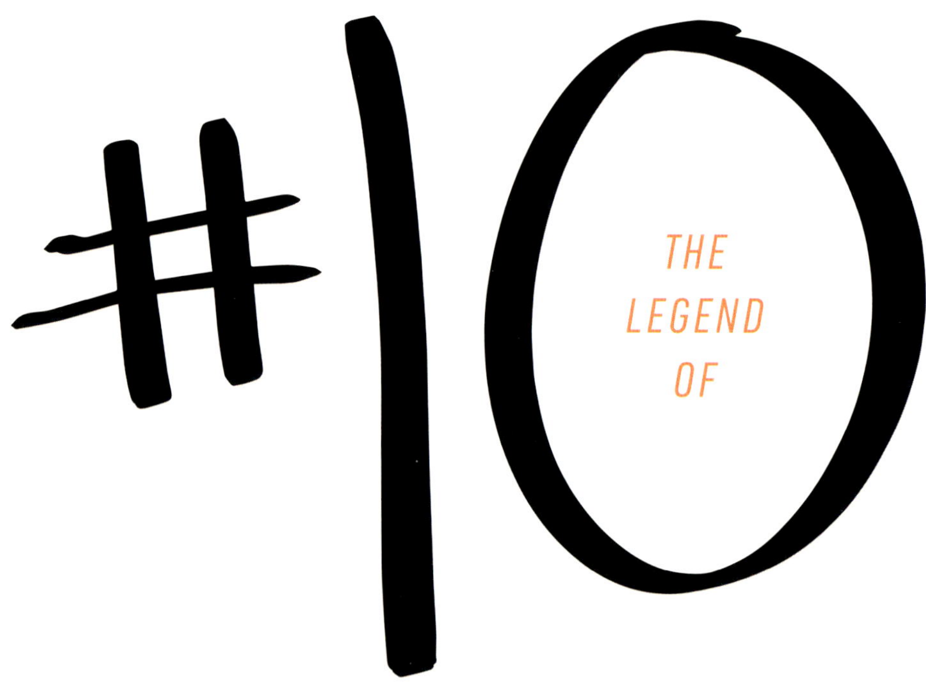

Pelé. Maradona. Totti. Platini. Messi. Zidane. Their names and achievements echo through the history of football, and on each one of their backs hung the number 10. The playmakers of the game have become synonymous with the number, and its origins have more to do with strategy than superstition.

In football's early years, jersey numbers were assigned by position. These squad numbers started with the goalkeeper at number 1, and moved up the field toward the wingers, midfielders, and forwards at numbers 7 through 11. As game strategy and formations evolved, some players dropped back, but the 9 and 10 players remained in front, positioned to take control of the game through their skill and creativity.

In the 1958 World Cup, the electrifying play of Pelé ignited the legend of number 10. The 17-year-old phenom exploded onto the world stage, scoring six goals in the tournament and leading Brazil to its first World Cup title. What seems serendipitous now, Pelé actually came upon his jersey number by accident. The Brazilian Football Confederation forgot to send the players' shirt numbers to the event, so Uruguayan official Lorenzo Villizzio chose to assign Pelé the number 10. Pelé led Brazil to two more World Cup titles, becoming one of the game's greatest players and sending fans clamoring for his famous jersey.

Diego Maradona's play as number 10 fanned the flames of the legend. Nicknamed "El Diez" or "D10S," a combination of the number 10 and the Spanish word for God, he was renowned for his dribbling, vision, and shotmaking. His strength and speed made him virtually unstoppable, forcing teams to foul him just to slow him down. In the 1986 World Cup, Maradona was fouled a record 53 times but still managed to score five goals and lead Argentina to a World Cup title. Lionel Messi once wrote, "Even if I played for a million years, I'd never come close to Maradona.... He's the greatest there's ever been." In 2000, FIFA named Pelé and Maradona the greatest players of the 20th century.

In today's game, jersey numbers are no longer assigned by position. By adorning so many greats over the years, the number 10 has amassed such significance that it is often awarded to a team's star offensive player, regardless of where they play on the field. It comes with respect and immense pressure to perform, which the great ones rise to meet.

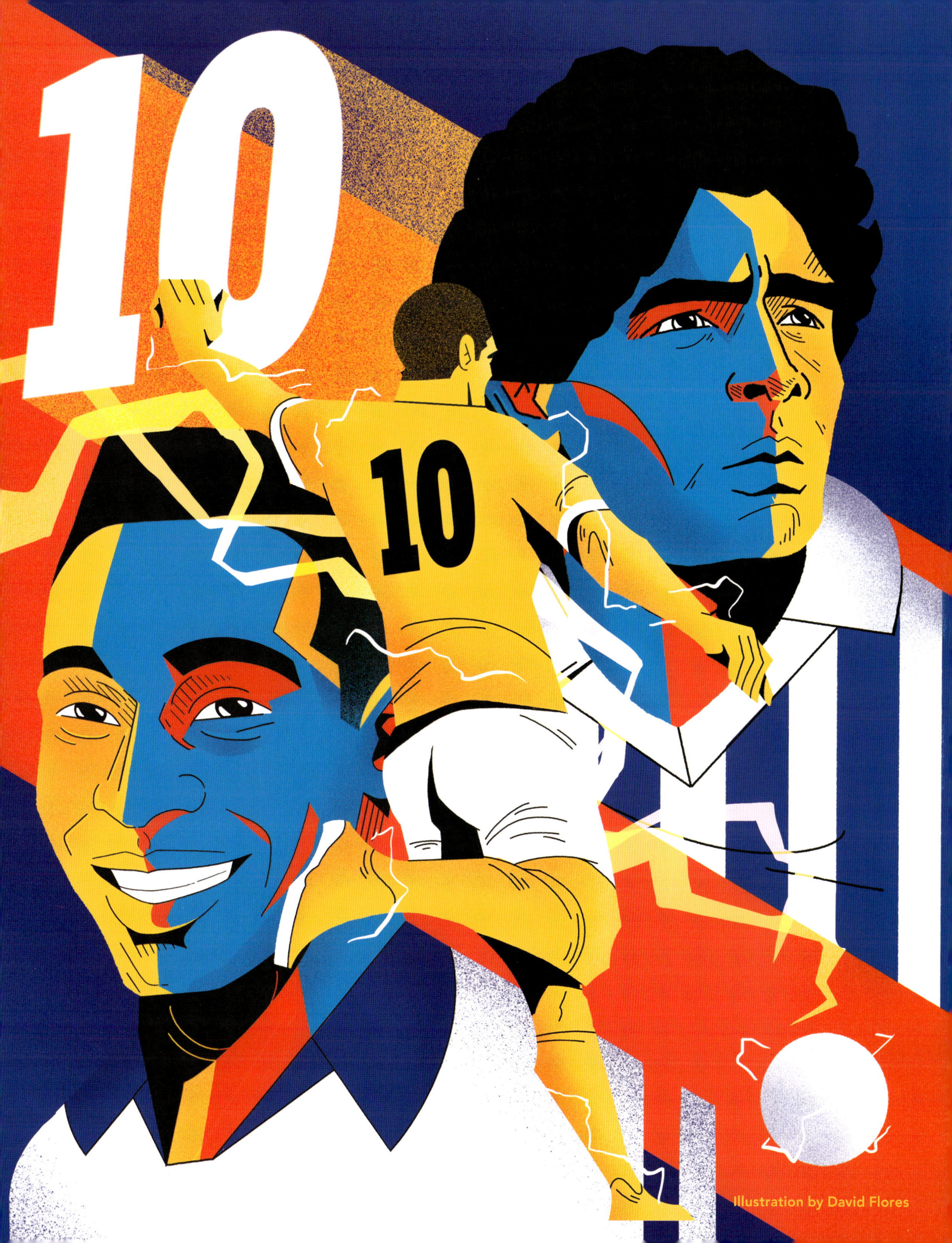

Illustration by David Flores

Paul Brown

In 1986, *Sport Magazine* wrote, "Paul Brown didn't invent the game of football. He was just the first to take it seriously." Brown's serious approach revolutionized coaching. He was the first to study film, scout talent, and grade players. He pioneered the use of assistant coaches, game plans, and practice squads. He invented the playbook, the face mask, and the helmet radio. "He wanted to control every single detail on the field. He wanted to know exactly what every player was going to do," said Mark Bechtel of *Sports Illustrated*.

Brown first implemented his ideas at the high school level, leading Ohio's Massillon Tigers to six state championships and four national titles. He then made the leap to college, coaching the Ohio State Buckeyes to a national championship in 1942. Brown's success made him a football legend in Ohio. In 1944, he was approached by businessman Mickey McBride, who was starting a football franchise in Cleveland. McBride offered Brown the coaching and general manager positions, and most importantly, complete control of the team. It was a deal Paul couldn't pass up. Brown's reputation and popularity bolstered the young franchise. When it came time to name the new team, McBride held a public poll, and the "Cleveland Browns" were born.

For the next decade, the Browns dominated. They reached the title game for 10 straight years, winning seven championships. But then Cleveland began to skid. In 1956, they had their first losing season. They bounced back in '57 and '58, but then slipped again the next few years. Brown was no longer winning consistently, and the players were frustrated with his rigid system. Paul was unwilling to change. He butted heads with new owner Art Modell, refusing to give up control of the franchise he built. Modell had the last word, firing Brown from his namesake team in 1963.

Five years later and 250 miles away, Brown set up a new franchise in Cincinnati, this time as majority owner. Brown coached the Cincinnati Bengals for eight seasons, but he never replicated the success he had in Cleveland. He harbored bad blood for his former team. Despite all the championships he won, when Cincinnati beat Cleveland for the first time, Brown called it "the greatest victory of my career." After coaching for 45 years, Paul Brown retired from football following the 1975 season. NFL commissioner Pete Rozelle said, "Whether they know it or not, nearly everyone in the game of football has been affected by Paul Brown."

"WHETHER THEY KNOW IT OR NOT, NEARLY EVERYONE IN THE GAME OF FOOTBALL HAS BEEN AFFECTED BY PAUL BROWN."

—PETE ROZELLE, NFL COMMISSIONER

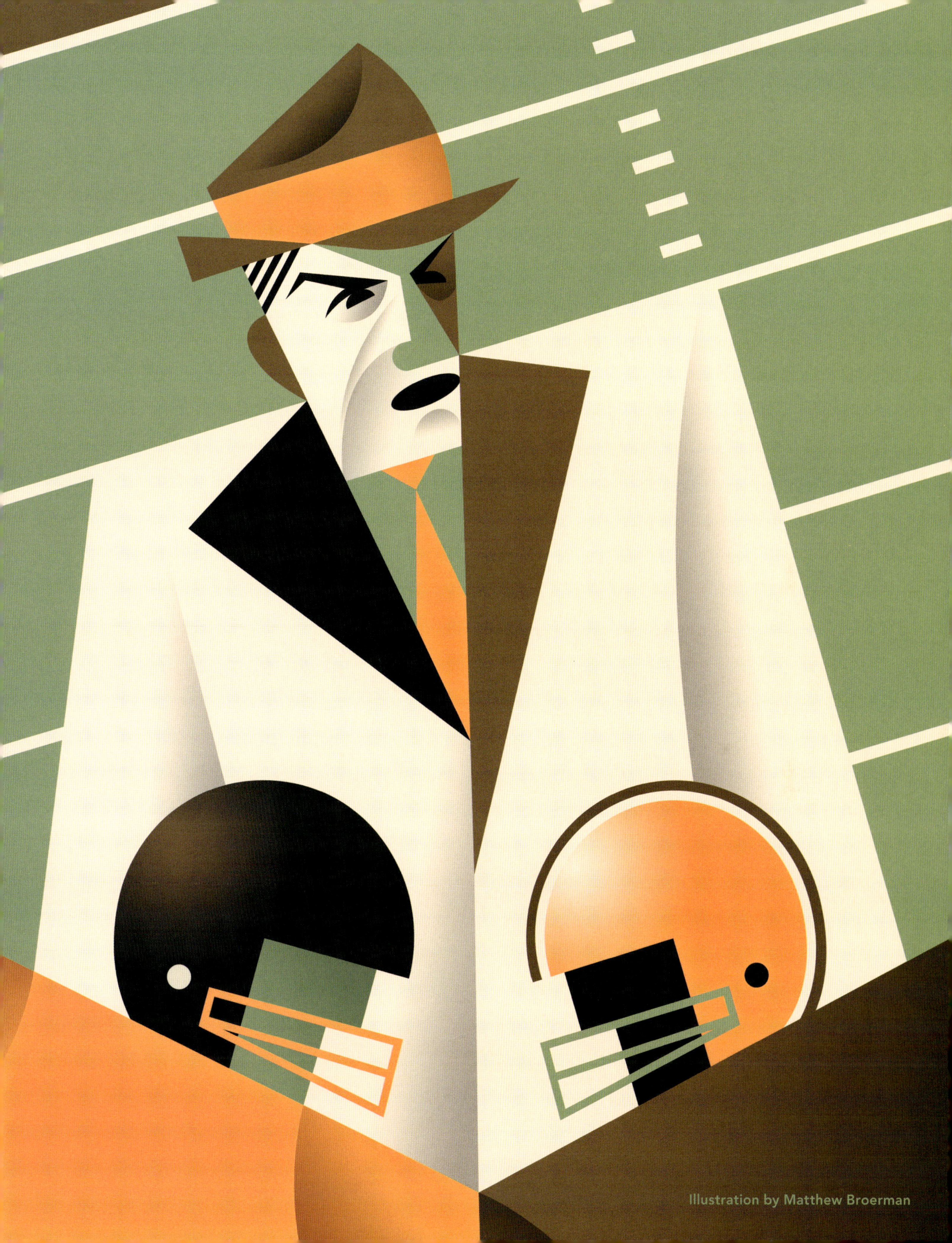

Illustration by Matthew Broerman

R.C. Owens

FIELD GOALTENDING

R.C. Owens wasn't the tallest player in football, but boy could he jump. The 6-foot-3 Baltimore Colts receiver was known for his acrobatic leaps and "alley-oop" catches. But on December 8, 1962, it wasn't a leaping catch that made headlines—it was something far more spectacular. In the first quarter of a game against the Washington Redskins, Washington kicker Bob Khayat was setting up for a 40-yard field goal attempt. Owens walked onto the field, but instead of heading to the huddle, he started trotting toward the goalpost. He set up like a goalie underneath the crossbar and awaited Khayat's attempt. The ball was snapped, the kick was up, and right before it passed through the uprights, Owens sprang from the ground and swatted the ball away.

The idea had come to Owens—or "Oop" as his teammates called him—in practice just a week earlier. "The kicker was kicking and I was shagging balls, and I jumped up there and blocked one," Owens said. "The coach came up to me after practice and said, 'Gee, whiz, Oop, we've got to put you in the game under the goalpost.'" R.C.'s famous block spawned imitators, none more imposing than 6-foot-10 Morris Stroud. Stroud was drafted in 1969 by the Kansas City Chiefs and head coach Hank Stram. Stram had a thing for tall players, once trying to sign 7-foot-1 NBA star Wilt Chamberlain to the Chiefs. "People thought I was kidding," Stram wrote. "Heck, I would have taken him in a second after seeing him handle a football." Stram recalled a mock tryout with Chamberlain, "I had him stand under the crossbar of the goalposts. I told him I was going to throw the football a little above the bar. The first throw touched the bar and bounced on over. Wilt asked me if I wanted him to start catching the ball... I threw again and he leaped up flat-footed and caught it." Unfortunately for Hank, Chamberlain already had a career, but Stroud was the next best thing. In fact, Morris didn't even play football in college. He was a basketball center, just like Wilt.

During field goal attempts, Stroud mimicked Owens, positioning himself underneath the goalpost. He came close to batting away a few attempts, but never connected. He tried it so often that the NFL eventually banned "goaltending" by any player trying to deflect a kick as it passed above the crossbar. The rule is informally known as the "Stroud Rule."

Morris Stroud

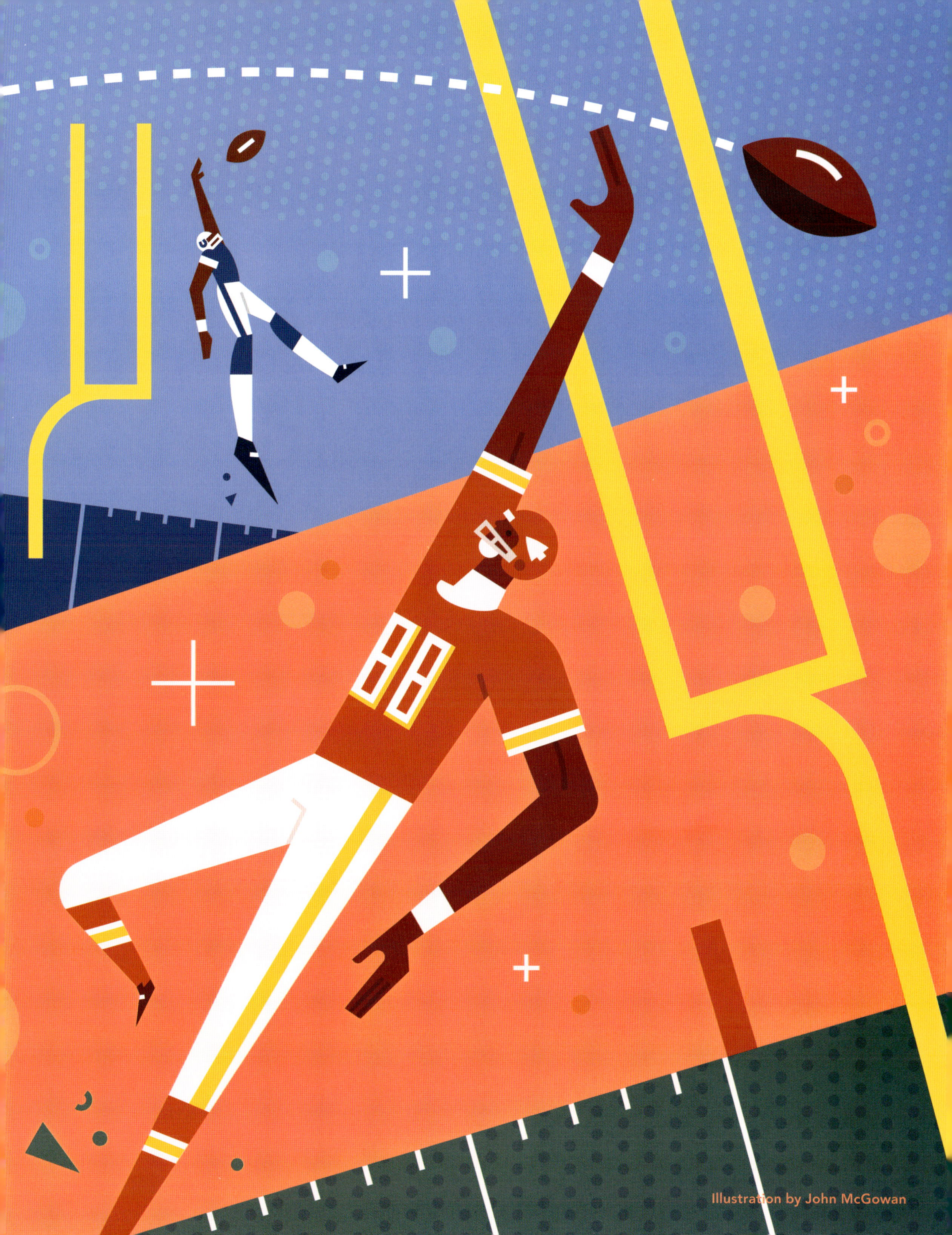

Illustration by John McGowan

Ray Mancini

A TRAGIC KNOCKOUT

On November 13, 1982, world lightweight boxing champion Ray "Boom Boom" Mancini stepped into the ring for a 15-round match with Korean boxer Duk-koo Kim. Kim was virtually unknown in the US, but he held the Orient and Pacific Boxing Federation lightweight title and had a record of 17-1-1. The pre-fight gossip was that Kim never backed down in the ring. Mancini hinted to sportswriters, "We're going to have a war."

As the bout started, "the fighters seemed united in their willingness to give and receive pain," wrote Mancini biographer Mark Kriegel. They exchanged flurries, each incurring injuries. Mancini suffered a torn ear. Kim took an uppercut to the heart. When the 13th round began, Mancini delivered 44 unanswered punches. Finally, Kim grabbed ahold of Mancini and slowed the onslaught. Ray broke free and pummeled him 17 more times. Kim retaliated with a series of body shots before the bell rang. Both gladiators were visibly drained. At the start of the 14th round, Ray charged out, delivering a beastly left hook and then a right to Kim's face. The Korean "fell as if blown back by an explosion," wrote Kriegel. He pulled himself up, only to collapse back on the ropes. Referee Richard Green immediately called the fight. Mancini, exhausted and battered, had won, 19 seconds into the 14th round. As he left the arena, he had no idea that his opponent was being carried off on a stretcher.

Kim fell into a coma, and doctors discovered a severe blood clot in his brain. He died four days later. The grief would take a heavy toll. Three months after the fight, Kim's mother died by suicide. Five months after that, referee Richard Green did the same. Mancini fell into a deep depression and lost his title. "In all the obvious ways, he was haunted," Kriegel said.

The devastating fight was a turning point for boxing, highlighting the dangers of the sport, especially in long bouts. Less than a month after Kim's death, the World Boxing Council announced that matches would be shortened from 15 to 12 rounds, setting a new standard. CNN reported a "steep decline in the number of fatalities following the death of South Korean lightweight Duk-koo Kim." In 2011, Mancini met with Kim's son, Chi-wan, to talk about that fateful day. During their conversation, Chi-wan said that he once felt "hatred" for Mancini, but now, 30 years after his father's death, Chi-wan told Ray, "I think it was not your fault."

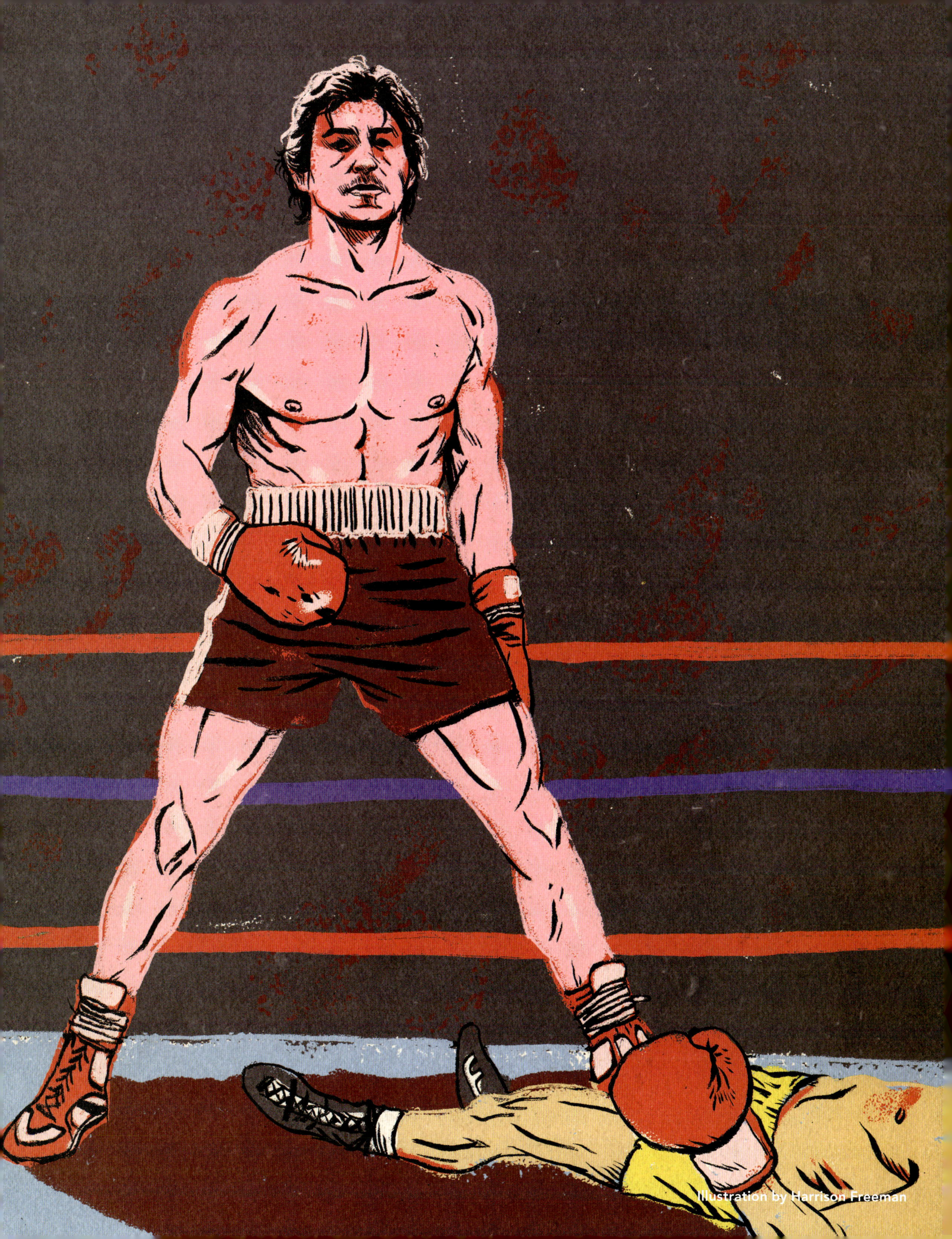
Illustration by Harrison Freeman

Robert Walter Johnson

The historic plaque outside of 1422 Pierce Street in Lynchburg, Virginia, reads, "The desegregation of tennis was due in large part to the efforts of Dr. R. Walter "Whirlwind" Johnson." It was here, at his home, that Dr. Johnson built a tennis court for Black players who weren't allowed to play on the White-only courts of the 1940s. Johnson was a successful physician and a prominent member of the Black community. He founded the Junior Development Program of the American Tennis Association as a way to give back to the community and share the game he loved with young Black players. But that wasn't his only motivation. Johnson was searching for talented Black athletes that he thought could break into the White world of professional tennis. In 1946, he found his first candidate.

While at an ATA tournament with fellow physician Dr. Hubert Eaton, Johnson spotted a young Althea Gibson. Tennis journalist Steve Tignor wrote, "She was all arms and legs, she was wildly erratic, and she didn't know much about tennis tactics, but she was among the most talented athletes they had ever seen." Johnson offered to train Althea during the summers, providing her food, lodging, and instruction for free at his Lynchburg home. "Who wouldn't be interested in a deal like that?" Gibson said. Johnson opened his home to dozens of Black athletes like Althea. He provided more than tennis coaching—he taught manners, grace, and etiquette. Johnson paid for everything. His students practiced all day Monday through Thursday, and on Fridays they drove to weekend tennis tournaments. He prepared his athletes to play tennis in a White-only world. Leslie Allen, a student of Johnson's, said, "He was preparing us for a world that didn't want us. If we could survive what he threw at us, we could survive anywhere." In 1950, Althea Gibson finally broke through the color barrier in professional tennis, competing in the US Nationals (now the US Open). Gibson went on to win five Grand Slam singles titles. Another Johnson student, Arthur Ashe, became the first Black man to win the US Open, the Australian Open, and Wimbledon. Ashe called Johnson, "my most powerful mentor."

Through his personal and financial sacrifice, Johnson earned the nickname the "godfather of Black tennis." In 2009 he was inducted into the International Tennis Hall of Fame. John McEnroe wrote of him, "Needless to say, our sport, our country, indeed the world community became a better place because of Althea and Arthur's achievements. Dr. Johnson made it possible for them to succeed."

"HE WAS PREPARING US FOR A WORLD THAT DIDN'T WANT US. IF WE COULD SURVIVE WHAT HE THREW AT US, WE COULD SURVIVE ANYWHERE."

—LESLIE ALLEN, JOHNSON'S STUDENT

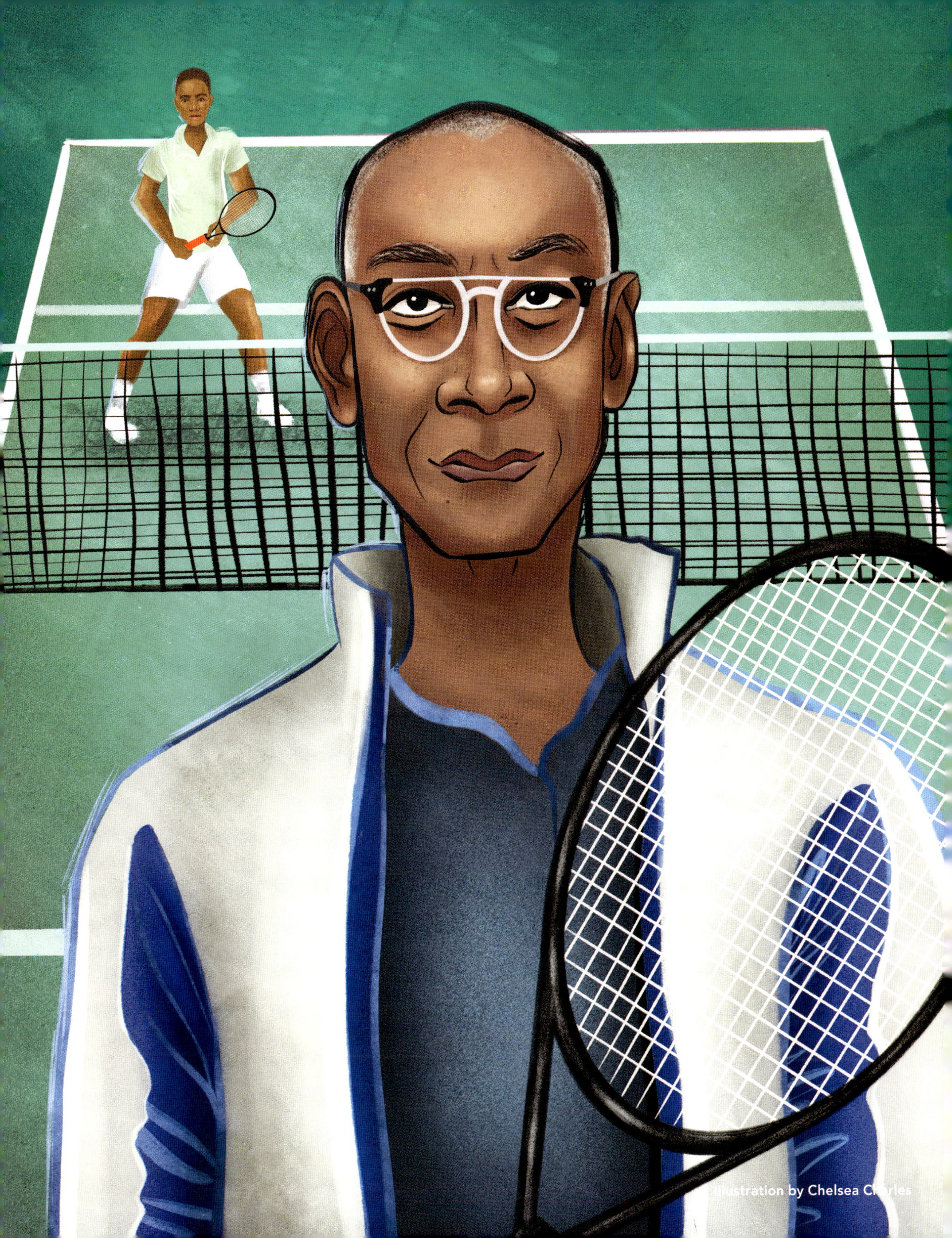
Illustration by Chelsea Charles

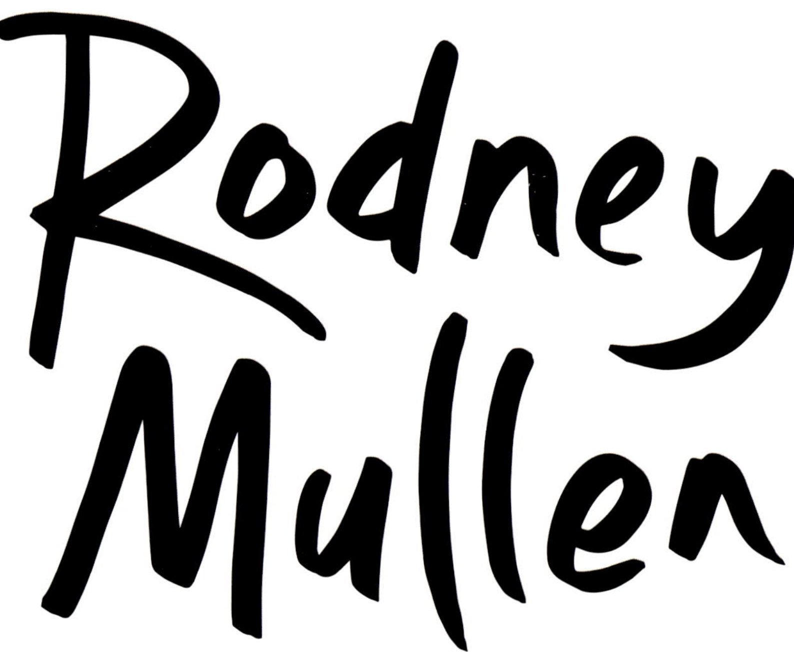

THE GODFATHER OF STREET SKATEBOARDING

"Without Rodney, skateboarding would still be in the dark ages," wrote *Transworld Skateboarding* in 2013. "After inventing the flatground ollie—in itself perhaps the most influential trick ever—he went on to unveil kickflips, backside flips, heelflips, 360 flips, double flips, impossibles, darkslides, and onward."

Far from the sidewalk-surfing skate culture of California, Rodney Mullen grew up as a shy kid in rural Florida. His strict father believed skateboarding was a waste of time, but he allowed Rodney to practice on the condition that he would quit if he got hurt. At the time, there were two types of skating: vert and freestyle. High-flying vert skaters soared off ramps, doing tricks in the air before coming back down. Freestyle skaters performed spins and balance moves while riding their boards on flat ground. The safety-minded Mullen chose freestyle. Covered in pads, he practiced day and night, alone in his family's garage. The isolation allowed him to create, expressing himself through his skating.

Mullen's freestyle was radically different from other skaters. He would ride on the side of the board, balance on the tail, flip it upside down, and spin it backwards. He used every edge of the board, stringing together trick after trick. In the late 1970s, Mullen began winning amateur skate events in Florida. He caught the eye of Tim Scroggs, another Florida skater and member of an elite skateboarding crew called the Bones Brigade. Tim urged the Brigade's manager, skate legend Stacy Peralta, to take a look at Rodney. Peralta was impressed, and immediately added Mullen to the crew. Over the next decade, the talented roster of the Bones Brigade—including Steve Caballero, Alan Gelfand, Tommy Guerrero, Tony Hawk, Mike McGill, Lance Mountain, and Rodney Mullen—dominated skating competitions, pioneering move after move. Mullen has been called the "godfather of street skateboarding" and is credited with inventing dozens of tricks. He attributed his originality to being isolated in Florida, practicing by himself in that garage. Mullen said, "I fell in love with skateboarding because it was individual; there were no teams, there were no captains, there was nothing to perfect. No style that had to be measured. It was completely opposite of what I saw in so many sports. It was creative. And to this day, that's what I love, that's always kept me back to it because it's endless creation."

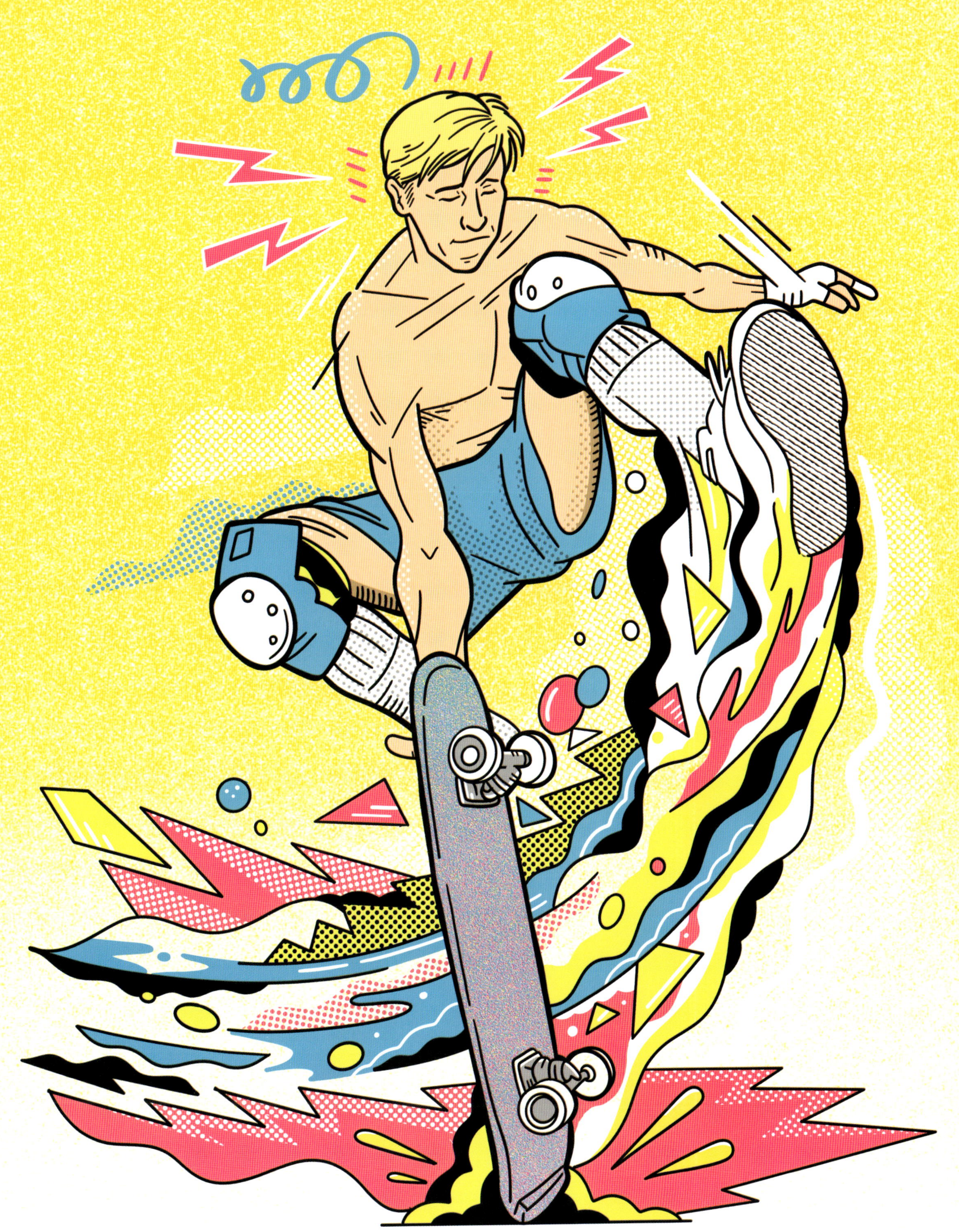

Illustration by Geo Law

Shaquille O'Neal

HACK-A-SHAQ

At 7-foot-1, 325 pounds, no NBA player had ever possessed the size, speed, and power of Shaquille O'Neal. If Shaq got the ball close to the rim, you could expect a dunk and maybe a broken backboard. There was nothing a defender could do to stop him—except foul. Like many big men before him, Shaq had one kryptonite. He couldn't shoot free-throws. Teams began intentionally fouling O'Neal to reduce his scoring, in a strategy known as "Hack-a-Shaq."

Dallas Mavericks coach Don Nelson pioneered the strategy in the late 1990s. The idea centered around fouling the worst shooter on the floor, whether they had the ball or not. A poor shooter would miss their free-throws, and the other team would gain possession. A similar tactic was used decades earlier against Wilt Chamberlain, another dominant big man with free-throw trouble. Wilt was often fouled at the end of close games as a way for opponents to stop the clock and get the ball back. Former NBA player and coach Pat Riley said some of the funniest things he ever saw were players chasing Wilt "like it was hide-and-seek." In 1966, the NBA decided to put an end to the shenanigans, creating a rule that fouls away from the ball during the last two minutes of a game would not result in a possession change. But in Shaq's case, he wasn't fouled in just the last two minutes. He was hacked all game long.

Nelson first tried the foul strategy against Dennis Rodman in a 1997 game. It didn't pay off, with Rodman hitting 9 of 12 free-throws. Two years later, Nelson tried it again, this time against O'Neal. Shaq made just 3 of 14 free-throws that game, and Hack-a-Shaq was born. San Antonio Spurs coach Gregg Popovich famously used the tactic in the 2008 playoffs against O'Neal's Phoenix Suns. Shaq went to the line 64 times that series, more than anyone else, but he made just 32 free-throws, the worst percentage of any player. The Suns lost the series in five games. Hack-a-Shaq became common throughout the NBA as a way to contain poor-shooting big men like O'Neal, Dwight Howard, and DeAndre Jordan.

When he retired in 2011, Shaq ranked fourth in all-time free-throw attempts, right behind Wilt Chamberlain. In 2016 the NBA finally altered the foul rule to discourage teams from using the strategy. Hack-a-Shaq undoubtedly affected O'Neal's numbers, but he still led the league in scoring twice, won four championships, and was a 15-time All-Star. Just imagine what he could have done if he hadn't been hacked.

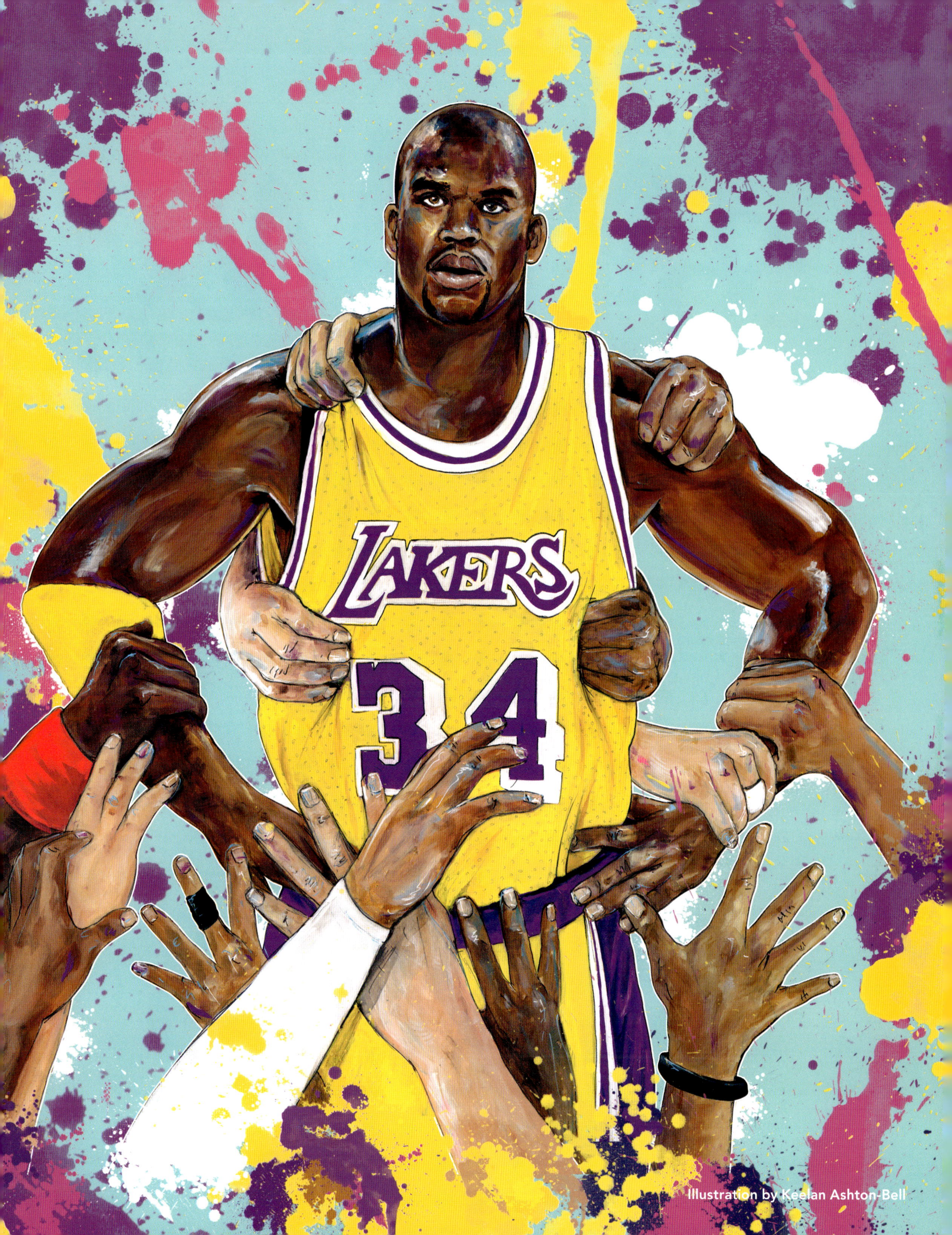

Illustration by Keelan Ashton-Bell

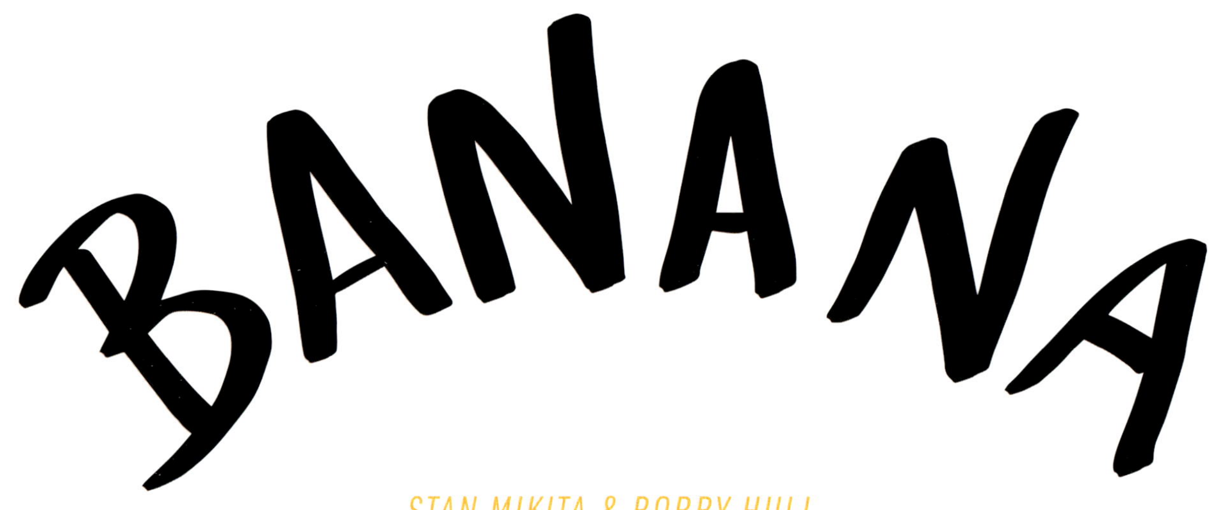

BANANA BLADES

STAN MIKITA & BOBBY HULL

Hockey's 1962 Chicago Blackhawks were anchored by two future Hall of Famers—Stan Mikita and Bobby Hull. Both were prolific scorers, but when Mikita accidentally created hockey's first "banana blade," it would take their scoring to record-setting levels.

In the 1960s, hockey players used sticks with flat blades, having no curve left or right. One day during a practice session, Mikita caught his hockey stick in a bench door and cracked the flat blade into a crooked V-shape. Not wanting to go all the way back down to the locker room for a new stick, he played on. "Mikita continued playing and to his surprise found that he could rip off a shot faster and harder with his crooked cudgel," wrote *Time* magazine in 1969. "Soon he and teammate Bobby Hull were warping the wooden blades of their sticks into scooplike curves by soaking them in hot water and wedging them under door jambs overnight."

Shots from the banana blades were a nightmare for goalies. The deep curve, sometimes almost three inches, led to pucks that were erratic and unpredictable. Glenn Hall, Chicago's goalie, was often on the receiving end of shots from Mikita and Hull during practice. Hall said, "We didn't like it.... The puck wasn't coming true."

Banana blades gave the Blackhawk stars an edge. Mikita had never been top 10 in points before the 1961-62 season, but from that season on, both he and Hull were top 10 in points for eight straight years. During three of those years, they finished first and second. In the 1968-69 season, Hull scored 58 goals, setting a new NHL record. Banana blades were great for scoring, but the irregular shots also made the game more dangerous. At the time, most players didn't wear helmets, goalies included. It was Mikita himself who would later advocate for helmets after a wayward puck tore off part of his ear in a December 1967 game. In 1970, the NHL voted 13-1 to limit the amount of curve on the blade to ½ inch, citing safety reasons. The one vote cast against the limit was Chicago Blackhawks coach Billy Reay. After 1970, Stan Mikita was never in the top 10 in points again.

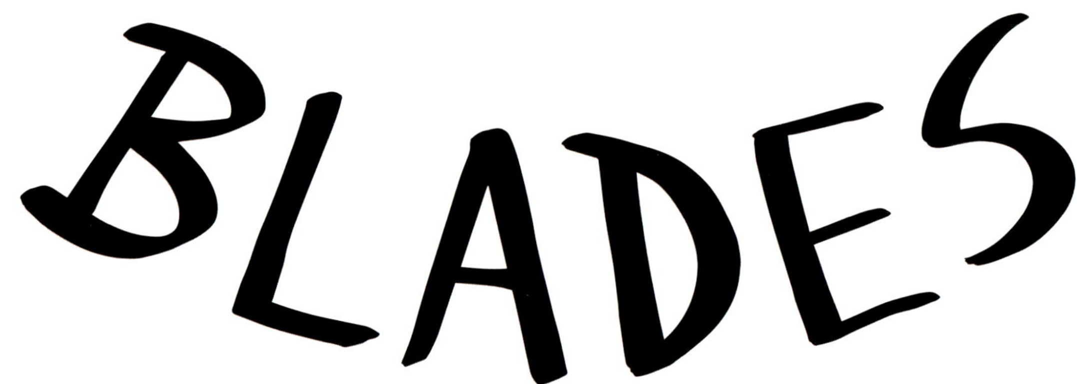

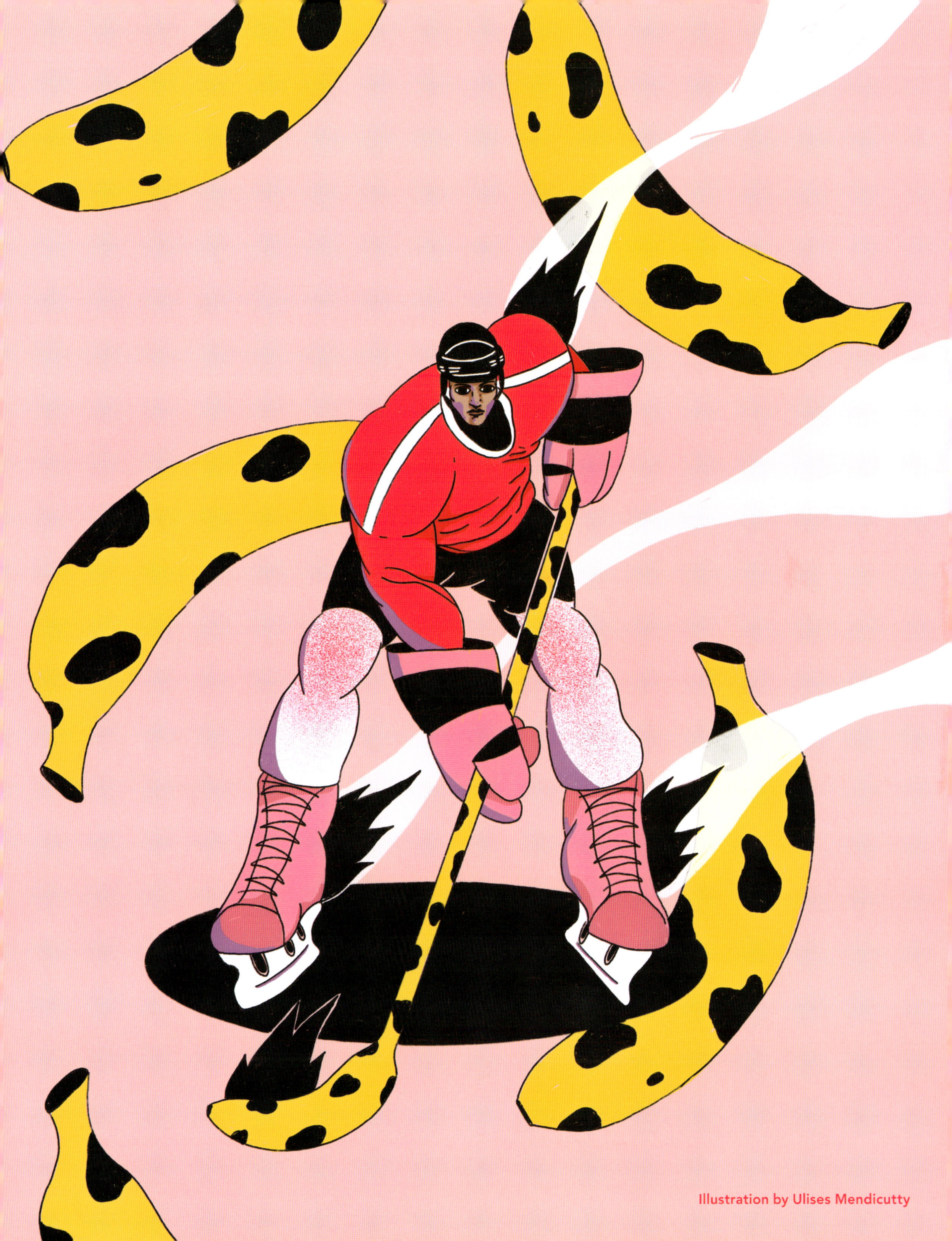

Illustration by Ulises Mendicutty

Stephen Curry

THE THREE-POINT REVOLUTION

On February 27, 2016, Steph Curry dribbled the ball down the floor with just five seconds left in overtime. The Golden State Warriors were tied with the Oklahoma City Thunder at 118 each. Curry took one dribble past halfcourt and launched a 37-foot bomb, 13 feet behind the three-point line. Before anyone knew what had happened, the shot dropped, winning the game for the Warriors. The crowd erupted, and Curry danced in victory.

Steph Curry ushered the NBA into a new era of long-range shooters and small-ball offenses. Emphasis on skill over size, points per possession, and player efficiency. The theory: if you make three points for every two that your opponent makes, there is no way they can win. Curry put the theory to the test. In 2012-13 he broke the single-season three-point record with 272. He broke it again two years later with 286. Then in 2015-16, he made an incredible 402 three-pointers, shattering his previous record. That same year he was selected as the first unanimous MVP in NBA history, and his Golden State Warriors set the record for most wins in an NBA season with 73.

As a deep threat from far beyond the arc, Curry took advantage of defenses. Over-eager defenders rushed to Curry and would either get blown away by his speed and ball-handling, or fall victim to a well-placed pass to another Golden State sharpshooter, Klay Thompson. Under-zealous opponents saw Curry take one or two dribbles past halfcourt and drop a devastating pull-up three, a shot he made famous. The rest of the league took notice, and the NBA transformed around Curry. Players like James Harden, Damian Lillard, and Trae Young are raining down more threes than ever before. Three-point attempts per season have doubled since 2012. Defenses are breaking as they need to guard players far beyond the arc, creating new offensive opportunities. In the 2018-19 season, teams averaged 13 more points per game than they did in 2012-13, the biggest six-year increase since the 1950s.

For decades, the NBA was dominated by big men, but today's game is different. Teams are winning with shorter lineups, emphasizing speed, shooting, and versatility. Steph Curry epitomized all three. He transformed the NBA style of offense, making the three-pointer a high-percentage shot. He built a dynasty with the Golden State Warriors, and he is considered by many to be the greatest shooter in NBA history.

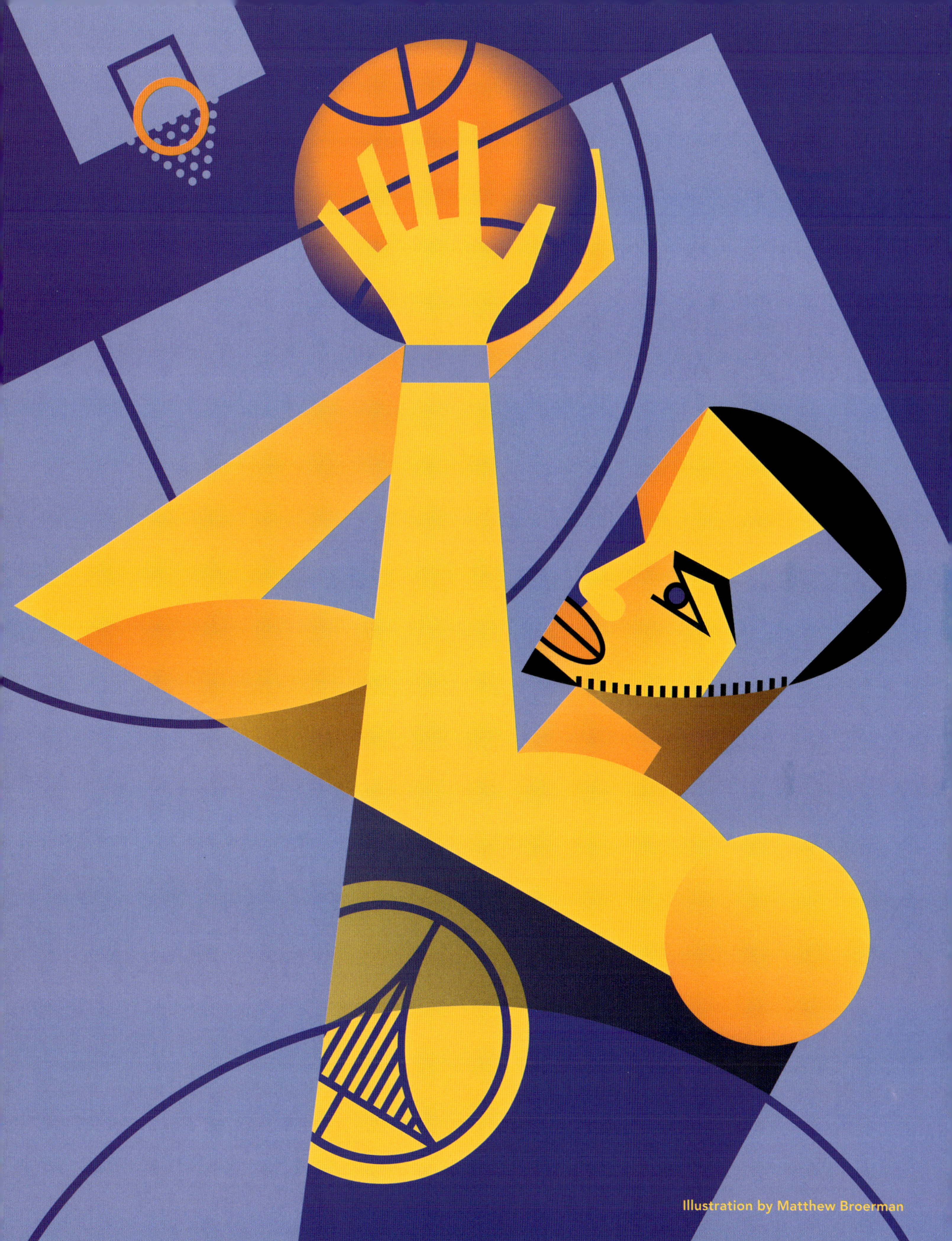

Illustration by Matthew Broerman

Tiger Woods

THE TIGER EFFECT

"I was embarrassed that I played golf when I was a kid," said PGA legend Jim Furyk. "It was not a cool sport to play." Tiger Woods changed all that. From the moment he burst onto the Tour in 1996, Woods captivated the public. With his 300-yard drives, pinpoint irons, and deft short game, he shattered records with swagger and gusto. He got his first win after just two months on Tour, and within a year, he was the world's number one player. Watching Woods dominate was must-see TV. At the 1997 Masters, Tiger shot a tournament-record 18-under par, beating his nearest competitor by 12 strokes. Runner-up Tom Kite said, "The Masters committee has to be a little concerned.... They've got a golf course that's pretty darn tough, and they've got somebody just ripping it up." Tiger won the Masters again in 2001, part of his streak of winning four consecutive majors, dubbed the "Tiger Slam." After his 2001 win, Augusta National, home of the Masters, made significant changes to the course layout, lengthening it in 2002 and again in 2006. During this time, many historic courses were "Tiger Proofing" by adding length to increase the difficulty for long hitters like Woods. Tiger's popularity had an even greater impact on the game. He became the blueprint for a new generation of golfer—one who spends as much time in the gym as on the course. Those who idolized Woods worked out, trained hard, and sought to mimic his skills and capture his essence. PGA champion Justin Thomas said, "I wore black pants and red shirt every tournament I played when I was a junior because of him." Soon, the gap between Woods and his competitors began to close. The average driving distance of today's PGA player matches Tiger's distance, once thought of as superhuman. After his 2019 Masters victory, Tiger described his influence, "A lot of the guys, especially on the Tour now, are training. They are getting bigger, stronger, faster, more athletic. They are recovering better. They are hitting the ball prodigious distances, and a little bit of that's probably attributed to what I did."

It took a generation, but PGA players have largely caught up to Woods. For a moment in the early 2000s, Tiger was untouchable. He was a man ahead of his time. He made the courses tougher, the competition better, and he drove the game forward with every swing.

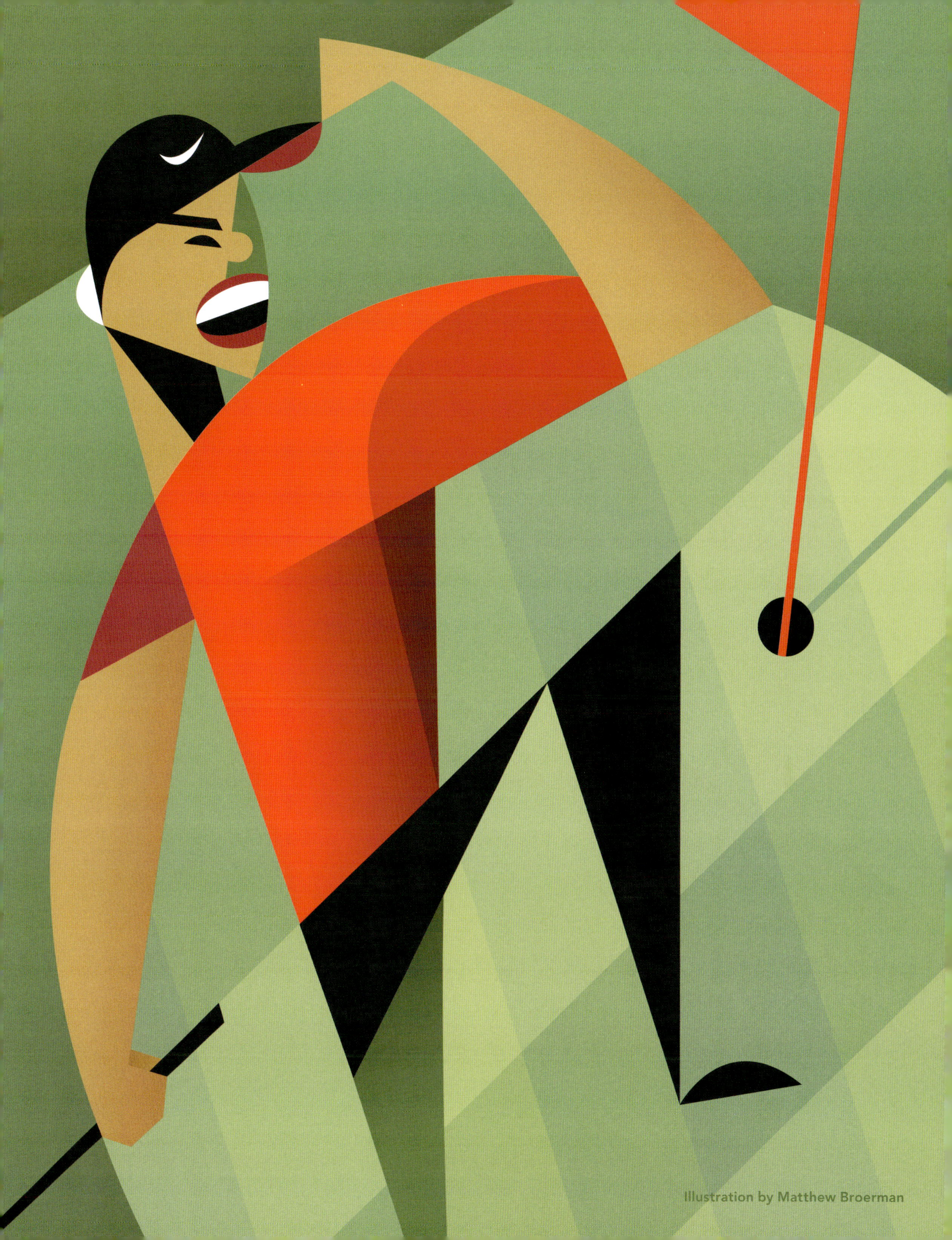

Illustration by Matthew Broerman

Tom Blake

Surf pioneer Tom Blake grew up in Midwest America, far from the salt and sand of the ocean. His mother died when he was a baby, and his father abandoned him shortly after, leaving Tom to float between relatives in Wisconsin and Minnesota. Growing up, he found solace in swimming the cool waters of Lake Superior. In 1918, he dropped out of high school and began drifting across the US. His wandering led him to Detroit and a chance encounter with legendary Hawaiian surfer Duke Kahanamoku. Tom was mesmerized by Duke's strength and aura. "As I look back now, I realize how much I was influenced by this first contact," Blake recalled. "Inspired by him, I took up swimming in earnest, after migrating to California later in 1920."

Blake supported himself as a lifeguard and became a champion swimmer. He tried surfing for the first time in 1921, but wiped out badly and quickly gave up. He tried again three years later and became enamored with the pastime. He picked up and moved to Hawaii, immersing himself in the history and culture. He befriended Duke and his family and spent his days swimming and surfing the Hawaiian shores. Blake remembered, "I was about the first mainlander to go over and actually live there and adopt their lifestyle." He became fascinated with the old surfboards at the Bishop Museum in Honolulu and was granted permission to study their design. Early surfboards were solid wood, weighing well over 100 pounds, and were difficult for even the strongest surfers to handle. Blake began experimenting with ways to make lighter boards. He tried drilling hundreds of holes in the solid wood and wrapping the board in veneer. This greatly reduced the weight, and Blake won the 1928 Pacific Coast Championship using this design. In 1932, he patented a hollow board built from a wooden frame covered in plywood. The hollow board weighed only 40 pounds, making it faster in the water but harder to control. Blake continued to tinker, adding the first fin in 1935. The lighter board and the added fin allowed surfers to turn in the water, transforming surfing into the sport it is today.

Blake lived his life as a surfing nomad, drifting between California and Hawaii. His blond hair, bronzed skin, and carefree attitude became the model for the American surfer. Sam George, editor of *SURFER* magazine, once wrote, "The extraordinary contributions of this one man to the lifestyle we call surfing are almost impossible to gauge. They're too broad, too all-encompassing... we still look like him, we still dress like him, we still surf like him."

"THE EXTRAORDINARY CONTRIBUTIONS OF THIS ONE MAN TO THE LIFESTYLE WE CALL SURFING ARE ALMOST IMPOSSIBLE TO GAUGE."

—SAM GEORGE, *SURFER* MAGAZINE

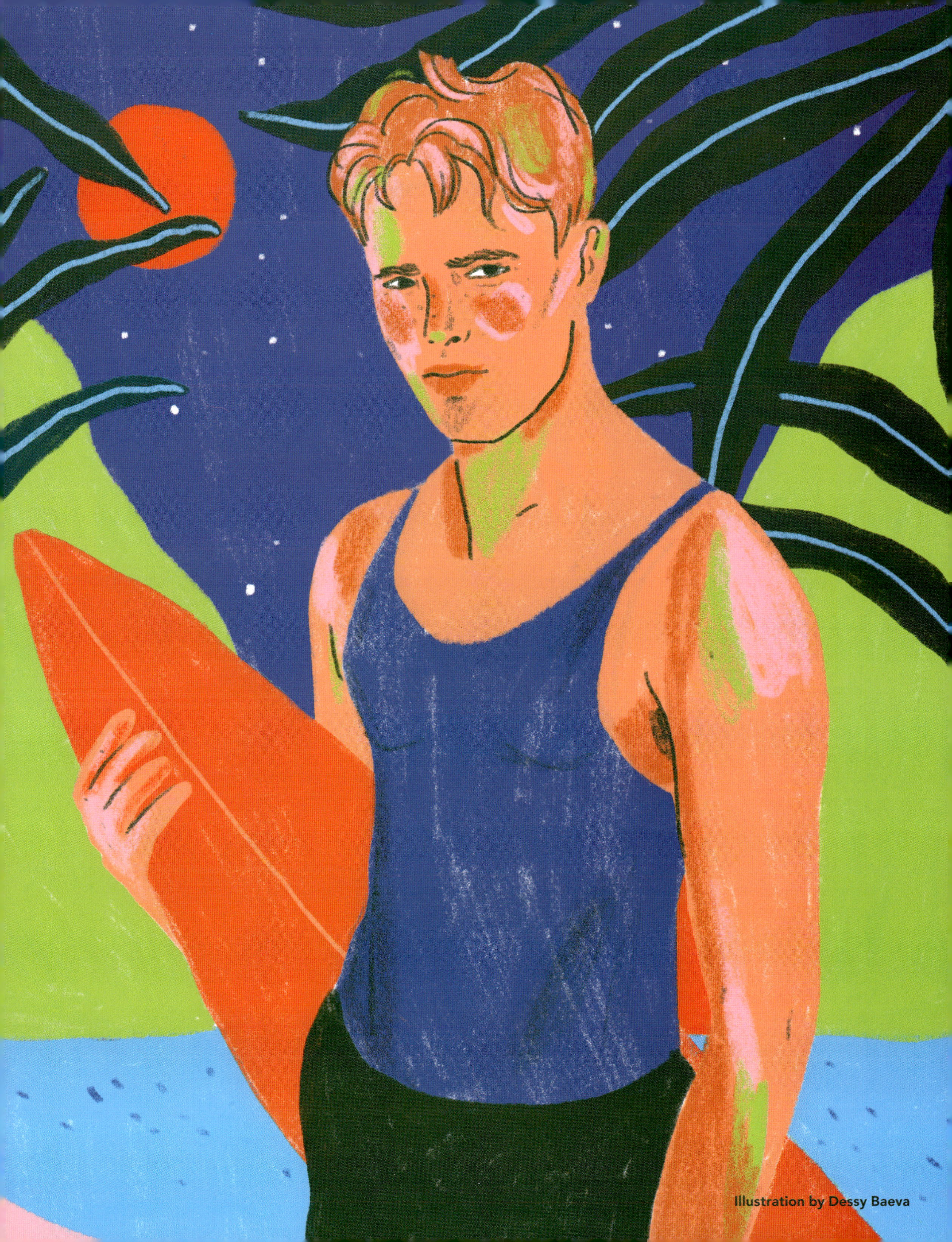

Illustration by Dessy Baeva

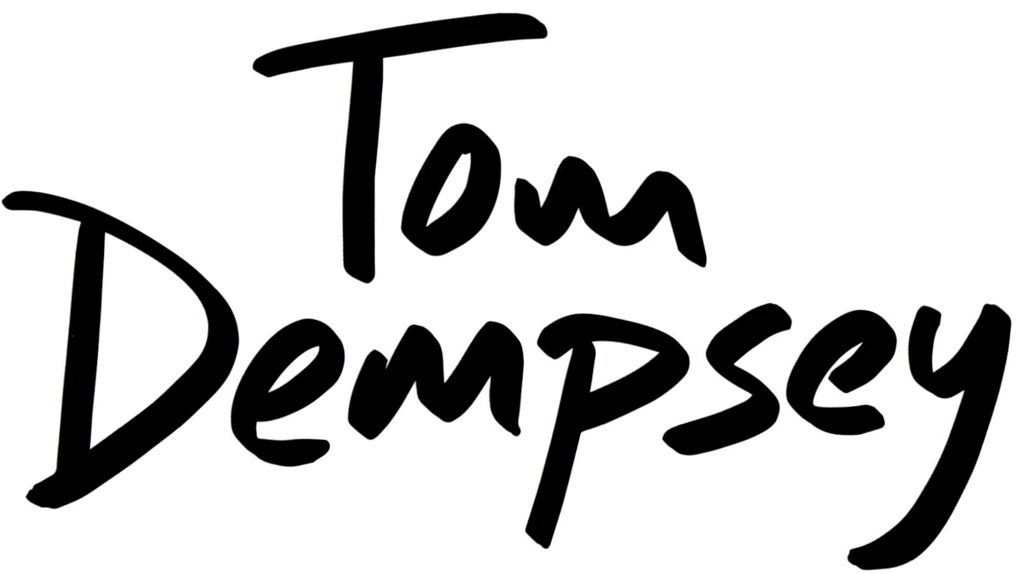

The New Orleans Saints didn't have much to cheer about in 1970. They were 1-5-1, on their way to one of the worst seasons in Saints history. On November 8, they were looking at another loss, down one point to the Detroit Lions with two seconds left in the game. The Saints needed a miracle. They sent out placekicker Tom Dempsey to attempt a 63-yard field goal, seven yards farther than the NFL record. Dempsey was unique among kickers in the NFL. He was huge, 6-foot-2 and 250 pounds. He was also missing all the toes on his kicking foot.

Dempsey wore a custom-built shoe with a flat front like a mallet. He was an erratic kicker, but he always gave it plenty of leg. "I knew I could kick the ball that far," he said, "but whether or not I could kick it straight that far kept running through my mind." Dempsey lined up his kick, and the ball was snapped. He took one step forward and swung his leg like a hammer. When Tom connected, holder Joe Scarpati said it sounded "like a cannon going off." As the ball tumbled through the air, announcer Don Criqui yelled, "I don't believe this! It's good! I don't believe it!" The Saints won 19-17, and Tom Dempsey celebrated into the New Orleans night.

While Dempsey partied, Dallas Cowboys president Tex Schramm was telling reporters that Dempsey had an "unfair advantage" because of the shape of his shoe. When the news broke, Dempsey replied, "Unfair, eh? How about you try kicking a 63-yard field goal to win it with two seconds left and you're wearing a square shoe, oh yeah, and no toes either." Schramm likened Dempsey's foot to the "head of a golf club," and his insensitive comments outraged the ACLU and other disability-rights groups. Tex claimed Dempsey had violated the rules, and as head of the NFL Competition Committee, he wanted something to be done. Dempsey countered, saying he was doing his best with the foot he was born with. The NFL ignored Schramm's pleas until 1977, when it instituted a new rule stating kickers must wear normal kicking shoes, regardless of the shape of their foot.

Dempsey said his father was responsible for his positive attitude toward his disability. His dad told him, "Boy, you never say can't. You may have to do it differently, but you can do it." Tom Dempsey, his record-breaking kick, and his iconic shoe are all commemorated in the New Orleans Saints Hall of Fame.

> "BOY, YOU NEVER SAY CAN'T. YOU MAY HAVE TO DO IT DIFFERENTLY, BUT YOU CAN DO IT."
>
> —HUEY DEMPSEY, TOM'S FATHER

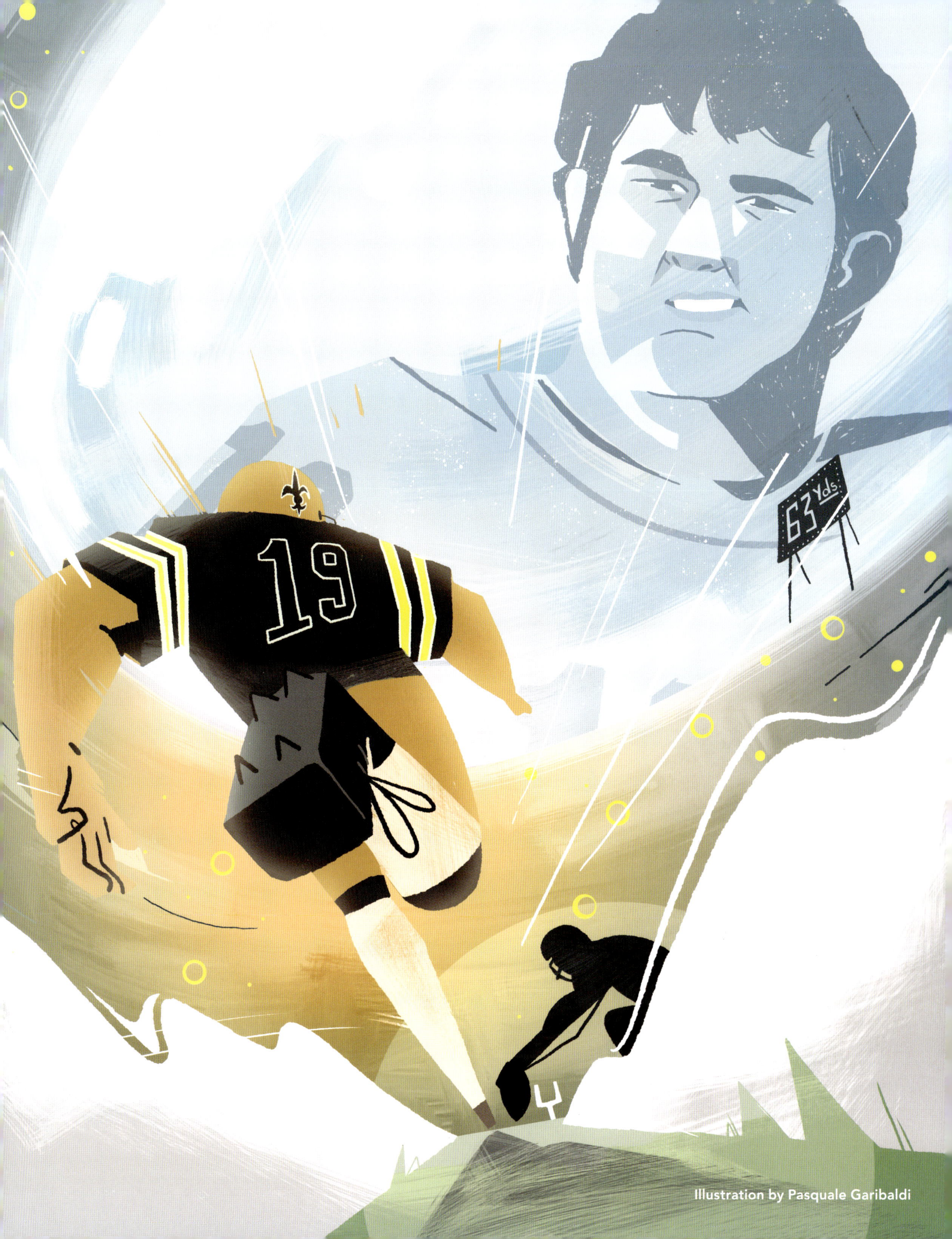

Illustration by Pasquale Garibaldi

"I THREW A SINKER AND RIGHT AS I THREW, I FELT THIS SEARING PAIN AND THE BALL JUST BLOOPED UP TO THE PLATE AND I WENT, 'HOLY MACKEREL, WHAT DID I DO?'"

—TOMMY JOHN

Tommy John

By his 12th major league season, left-handed pitcher Tommy John had already built a respectable career. He was an All-Star. He had 124 career wins. And halfway through the 1974 season, he was 13-3, the best record in the National League. On July 17, he went for his 14th win as the Los Angeles Dodgers faced the Montreal Expos. In the third inning, John threw a pitch, and his arm went dead. He recalled, "I threw a sinker and right as I threw, I felt this searing pain and the ball just blooped up to the plate and I went, 'Holy mackerel, what did I do?'" John attempted another pitch with the same result. "I got to the bench, I got my jacket and I told our trainer, I said 'Billy, let's get Dr. Jobe—something's wrong.'"

Dr. Frank Jobe was the Dodgers team surgeon. He diagnosed Tommy John's arm with "overuse syndrome" and recommended resting it. After a few weeks, John tried to throw again and couldn't even get the ball to home plate. X-rays revealed that John had ruptured his ulnar collateral ligament (UCL), and without surgery, his career was over. When John met with Dr. Jobe again, the doctor suggested a radical new procedure to reconstruct Tommy's left elbow. The operation involved drilling holes in the elbow and weaving a tendon from another part of the patient's body—in this case John's right wrist—through the holes to form a new ligament. After laying out the approach, Dr. Jobe remembered John's reaction. "He looked around my office very seriously. He looked me in the eye and said, 'Let's do it.'" John underwent surgery on September 25, 1974. The Dodgers went to the World Series that year, and John was on the bench in his cast, cheering for his team. Eighteen months later, he was back on the mound.

What seemed like a career-ending injury at the time turned out to be the opening scene in a second act. Post-surgery, John pitched for an amazing 14 more seasons. He won 164 more games, was selected as an All-Star three more times, and pitched in three different World Series. His 26 seasons as a pitcher in the majors is second only to Nolan Ryan. "Tommy John Surgery" became the common name for the UCL reconstruction procedure pioneered by Dr. Frank Jobe. The surgery is now regularly performed on major league pitchers, turning a once career-ending injury into a chance to make a comeback as spectacular as Tommy John's.

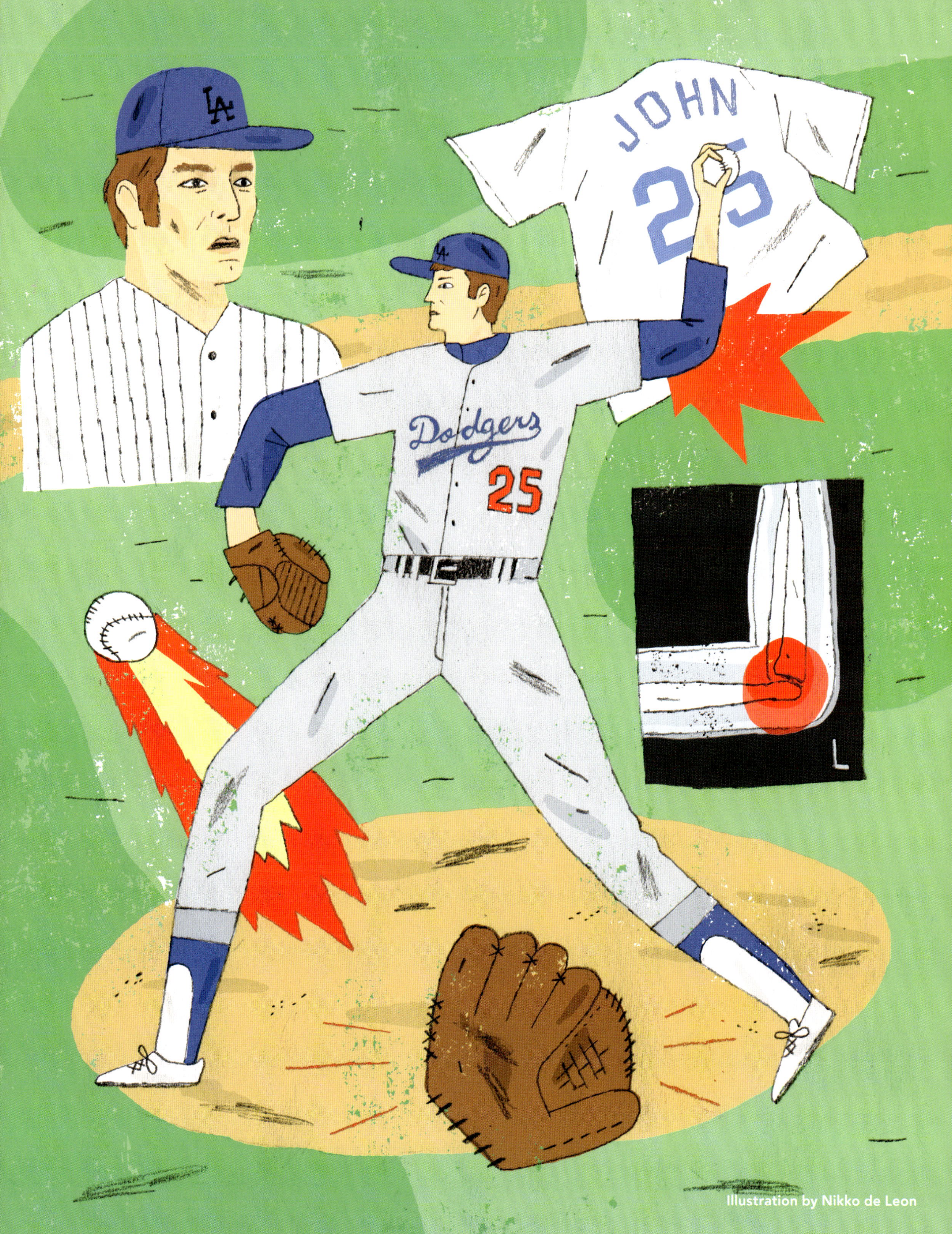

Illustration by Nikko de Leon

Usain Bolt

THE WORLD'S FASTEST MAN

At the 2009 World Championships, 6-foot-5 Jamaican sprinter Usain Bolt ran the 100-meter dash in 9.58 seconds, setting a new world record. Of all the athletes who held the title "world's fastest man," no one had been bigger than Bolt. His speed dumbfounded competitors and made coaches and researchers reevaluate the science of biomechanics. World-class sprinters were supposed to be powerhouses of fast-twitch muscles in compact bodies. How could Usain be so tall and so fast?

Scientists have been trying to understand Bolt's speed since he set his first world record in 2008. Researchers believe sprinters with long legs may have an advantage once they get to top speed. The average human takes around 55 strides to run 100 meters, while elite sprinters take about 45 steps. Bolt took 41. "Stride length is the biggest determinant between a good sprinter who's able to run under 10 seconds and those sprinters who can't," said former Olympic sprinter Craig Pickering. Bolt was the latest in a trend going back more than a century. Sprinters have been getting bigger and faster. At the 1900 Olympics, 5-foot-5 Frank Jarvis took home gold in the 100-meters with a world-record time of 10.8 seconds. Jarvis was 12 inches shorter and 1.2 seconds slower than Usain Bolt.

If the trend continues, is there a limit to how fast a human can run? "It is impossible to run 9.2," Bolt himself stated. "The body isn't made to go that fast no matter how hard you train, how good a shape you're in or how good your technique." Some scientists disagree.

Peter Weyand, a physiologist at Southern Methodist University, argued that speed is a combination of stride frequency and the amount of force a runner applies to the ground with each step. Larger sprinters generate more force. Bolt generated about 1,000 pounds of force with each step, but Weyand argued that the human leg is capable of so much more. In 2010, he conducted an experiment asking participants to jog, run, or hop on one foot while on a treadmill. Hopping generated 30% more ground force than running, and Weyand theorized that if a sprinter ran each step with the hopping force, they could run the 100-meters in 5.18 seconds! While that may prove impossible, most scientists agree that we have not yet reached the human speed limit. For now, Usain Bolt is the fastest there has ever been. He electrified fans with his size, speed, and charisma, and set off a scientific race to find out just how fast a human can run.

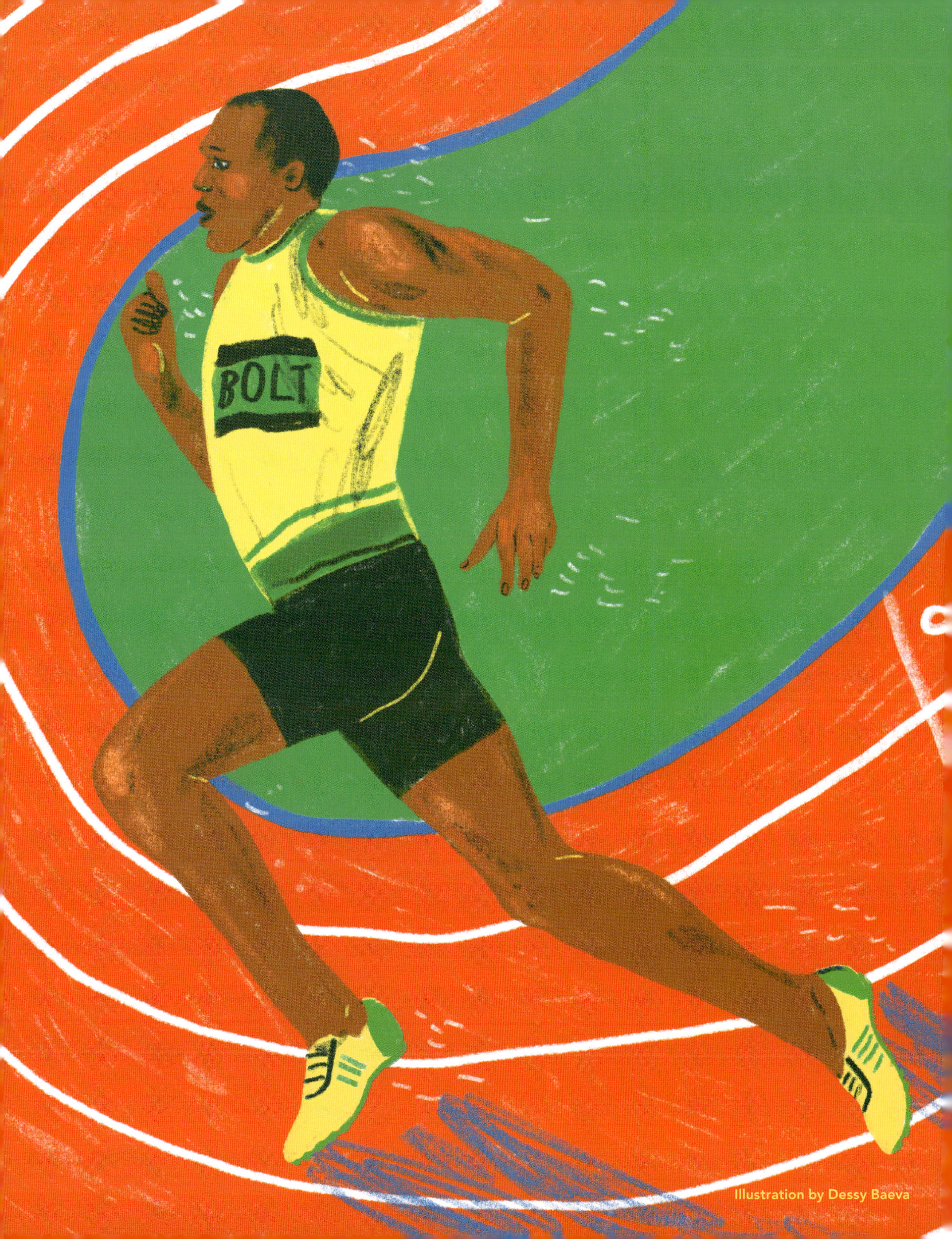

Illustration by Dessy Baeva

"EVERYBODY PULLS FOR DAVID, NOBODY ROOTS FOR GOLIATH."

—WILT CHAMBERLAIN

Wilt Chamberlain

At 7-foot-1, 275 pounds, Wilt Chamberlain was an imposing presence on the basketball court. His size, speed, and strength allowed him to do things no other player could. He could jump from the foul line and dunk the ball. He could snatch a quarter off the top of the backboard, 13 feet in the air. Critics argued it was unfair, saying he would ruin the game of basketball. Wilt countered, "Everybody pulls for David, nobody roots for Goliath."

Even before he played his first varsity game at the University of Kansas, opposing coaches were discussing ways to stop Wilt. Rival Kansas State coach Tex Winter was particularly concerned about the gifted giant, saying, "Look... we have to play that big guy for the next three years." In 1955, Tex attended a scrimmage to see Chamberlain in action. That was the first time he saw Wilt dunk a free-throw. "He wasn't at the top of the circle, but he was about three steps behind it," Winter recalled. "He ran to the free-throw line, took off and dunked the ball." Tex couldn't believe his eyes. He was outraged, and he had to do something. Fortunately for him, he had been appointed chairman of the Coaches Rules Recommendation Committee for the upcoming year. If he could convince the committee, Tex could change the rules and outlaw the flying free-throw before Kansas and Kansas State ever stepped on the floor. At the 1956 NCAA convention, Tex pleaded his case, "I explained to the coaches at the convention what I saw and said something's got to be done." SMU coach Doc Hayes called what Chamberlain was doing "cheating." The rest of the committee agreed, and by the end of the convention, they had changed half a dozen rules, many targeting Wilt. They banned dunking foul shots, inbound passes over the backboard, and created a new rule for offensive goaltending. The NBA soon followed suit with similar additions to their own rulebook.

The changes had little effect on Chamberlain's stellar career. In the NBA, he led the league in scoring for six straight years, won four MVPs, and two championships. In 1962 he scored an unbelievable 100 points in a single game, still an NBA record. Many consider him the greatest player of all time. In 1997, before a ceremony honoring the NBA's best, Wilt Chamberlain met Michael Jordan for the first time. The two greats soon began discussing who was better. Wilt ended the conversation saying, "Just remember, Michael, when you played, they changed the rules to make it easier for you to dominate. When I played, they changed the rules to make it harder for me."

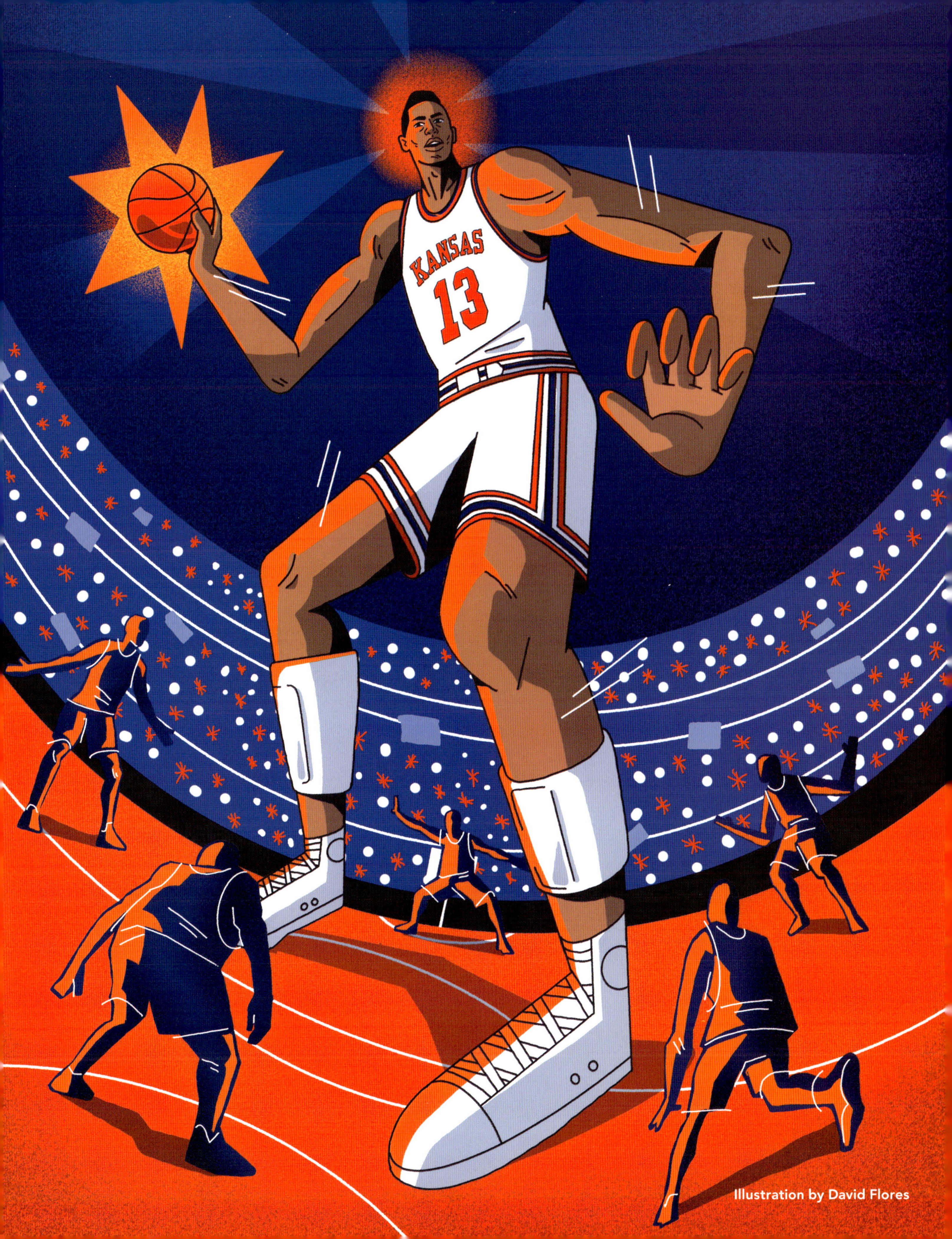

Illustration by David Flores

ILLUSTRATORS

CHELSEA CHARLES, CANADA (25, 89)
chelseacharlesillustration.com

CLÉMENT SOULMAGNON, FRANCE (31, 73)
instagram.com/clement_soulmagnon

DAVID FLORES, MEXICO (45, 81, 109)
instagram.com/elchiak

DAVID LOMELI, USA (51, 59)
flyingdork.com

DESSY BAEVA, UK (101, 107)
dessybaeva.com

ELENA HORMIGA, SPAIN (13, 35, 65)
elenahormiga.es

GEO LAW, UK (23, 33, 91)
getaloadageo.co.uk

HARRISON FREEMAN, USA (29, 71, 87)
harrisonfreeman.com

JOHN McGOWAN, USA (85)
instagram.com/johmcgowan

JULIE HILL, USA (67)
julie-hill.com

KEELAN ASHTON-BELL, AUSTRALIA (75, 93)
killustrate.net

LARA PAULUSSEN, GERMANY (19)
larapaulussen.de

MARIE MURAVSKI, RUSSIA (57, 63)
mariemuravski.works

MATTHEW BROERMAN, USA (21, 55, 83, 97, 99)
inkandcraft.com

MICHAEL RENDELL HENSLEY, USA (41)
instagram.com/blackhorse.creative

NATE SWEITZER, USA (15, 47, 53, 79)
instagram.com/natesweitzer

NIKKO DE LEON, USA (17, 39, 77, 105)
nikkothelion.com

PASQUALE GARIBALDI, ITALY (37, 103)
pasqualegaribaldi.com

SARAH DAHIR, SOUTH AFRICA (11, 61)
instagram.com/nawaal_illustrations

ULISES MENDICUTTY, SPAIN (95)
mendicutty.com

YAGIZ YILMAZ, TURKEY (43)
yagizout.com

ZACHARIAH STUEF, USA (27, 49, 69)
stuefcreative.com